A. D.

WHO IS THE
RADICAL
ISLAMIST?
AND WHY?

outskirts
press

Who Is the Radical Islamist? and Why?
All Rights Reserved.
Copyright © 2018 A. D. Simmons
v7.0

The opinions expressed in this manuscript are solely the opinions of the author and do not represent the opinions or thoughts of the publisher. The author has represented and warranted full ownership and/or legal right to publish all the materials in this book.

This book may not be reproduced, transmitted, or stored in whole or in part by any means, including graphic, electronic, or mechanical without the express written consent of the publisher except in the case of brief quotations embodied in critical articles and reviews.

Outskirts Press, Inc.
http://www.outskirtspress.com

ISBN: 978-1-4787-9450-9

Library of Congress Control Number: 2017919138

Cover Photo © 2018 thinkstockphotos.com. All rights reserved - used with permission.

Outskirts Press and the "OP" logo are trademarks belonging to Outskirts Press, Inc.

PRINTED IN THE UNITED STATES OF AMERICA

TABLE OF CONTENTS

INTRODUCTION

I developed a deep interest in the radical Islamist movement of the early 1980s when I started tracking and gathering information on the young mujahidin who had left their families and communities to become part of their fellow Muslim brotherhood to free Afghanistan from the Soviet Union. These young men were very loyal to Usama bin Laden and eager to fight and to prove their dedication as "warriors of Allah." They proved not only to themselves but also to many other young men throughout the universal Muslim *ummah* that Allah once again was on their side and now was the time to rectify all past humiliation/loss of face. A small group of dedicated Muslim warriors had forced a world super power to retreat and fall. I soon discovered that it was this young dedicated "brotherhood" that had developed into an international movement with strong connections with the Egyptian Muslim Brotherhood organization. My research soon uncovered information not only as to where these young men were now living but also how they had become indoctrinated into the radicalized movement and had become such a ruthless and brutal global militia force. I also discovered that they had kept in contact with bin Laden and with each other. This new brotherhood, "the base," had formed under the leadership of Usama bin Laden and trained in his organized militia training camps and had established sleeper cells within their homelands. I developed a passion to continue my research and to uncover their movements and their revival of the seventh century radical Islamic movement.

Numerous friends, colleagues, and my late parents kept prompting me to write a book about my experiences, studies, and research of Islam and the radical Islamist movement. History has revealed various radical movements that have evolved from Christianity, Judaism, and Islamic individuals and groups that do not represent all of their adherents but who have used various verses from their sacred texts to justify their beliefs and behaviors. I wish to make it very clear that the pages within this book deal only with the twenty-first century radical Islamic movement and answers the following questions: who is the radical Islamist, and why do they do what they do? To provide validity and credibility to my argument I have supported my conclusions with quotes from (1) the Holy Qur'an published by the King Fahd Holy Qur'an Printing Complex, in Mecca, Saudi Arabia; (2) the sacred words and deeds of the Prophet Muhammad, peace be upon him, as recorded by Sahih Al-Bukhari (who is recognized by both the Sunni and the Shiite as a creditable source); (3) numerous radical Islamist documents confiscated during US and foreign government intelligence raids; (4) evidence, testimonies, and documents recorded from terrorists and/or terrorism from related court trials; (5) recorded interviews of radical Islamic leaders posted by international media; (6) literary manuscripts and books written by radical Islamist scholars, Imams, and leaders; (7) posted international media coverage of their staged carnage propaganda postings; and (8) personal interviews of 225 individuals, US and foreign,

Muslim and non-Muslim, from various walks of life and ranging in age from eighteen to ninety-eight.

What is important to underline at the outset of this book is that there is no one international definition of terrorism; therefore, there is no common international law or an international court in which terrorists can be tried. The United Nations has defined slavery, piracy, and genocide, but has refused to establish an international legal definition of terrorism. Numerous conferences have been established that define various acts of terrorism, but as of the date of publication of this book every nation is left on its own to establish a definition of terrorism and to try the captured terrorists—hence the confusion and friction found not only between nations but also within nations as to who radical Islamist terrorists are and how they are to be tried.

This book disputes the conception that the twenty-first century radical Islamist is a "new breed" of terrorist and that there are no historical evidence or documents that can aid in researching and developing a true counterterrorism strategy. It is this misconception that enticed me to write this book, and why it became such a personal passion and commitment over the years to explain and define not only -Who the twenty-first century radical Islaimist is but also Why they do what they do.

As you can guess, I was an oddity in the eighties and nine-ties in the field of the Arab/Islamic culture and mind-set and in the studies of the development of a multinational terrorism movement. Because of this oddity I have faced many confron-tations, ridicule, and yes, even resentment in my twenty-seven plus years of studying, working and living within this fantastic and deep historical arena. I was an oddity because I not only disagreed with this general conception but also because I had chosen, in the very beginning of my career, to learn the true Arab and Islamic culture and mind-set, which meant actually studying, living, working and engrossing myself in their culture and world. It was this decision that has provided me a broader understanding of not only their mind-set but an understanding and respect for their three sacred texts: the Holy Qur'an, the sayings of Muhammad recorded in the *Sunnah* ("a path" or "a way"), and his deeds recorded in the *Hadith* and the Divine Law of Allah—*Shari'ah* law. My greatest memories are the opportunities I had to listen to stories that had been passed down from generation to generation of their tribal victories, their ancestors' survival in the geographical phenomena of the region, and the major role Muhammad played in the development of Islam, the region, and their thousand-year-old heritage. Stories that expressed their great pride, and those that expressed their humiliation and loss of face from their fall after the Islamic "Golden Age of Islam," to numerous battles and struggles they had to endure because of the crusaders and Mongolian invasions, and their major losses of both territory and culture of pride because of WWI and WWII. This was an experience that has offered me the opening of numerous doors for research into the advancement of a movement that was influencing both the Muslim and non-Muslim citizens in this region and the world. It is by this intercultural personal learning experience that I perceived the radical Islamist movement not to be a new breed but rather a revival based on tradition (*tijdid*). Shortly after Desert Storm I predicted that the American counterintelligence and the FBI would be faced with combating American homegrown Islamic terrorists and a very powerful and effective movement of infiltration by the Islamic movement within the country's infrastructure. Both of my predictions have been proven to be true but unfortunately both caused me to be 'blackballed' from lecturing and working in various US government organizations and training facilities. For example, I was invited to lecture to a group of high-ranking military and government personnel who were representing America in the building and establishing of a fully operational and functional airstrip and facility for the American military in Uzbekistan, located in Central Asia. This strategic project, which the Uzbekistan government had invited America to build, was to serve as both a hub for the American military support and as a hub for the humanitarian missions to Afghanistan and the region. During my lecture I was asked several questions in reference to this project and what I would predict of its success. I hesitated for a moment and asked if these were loaded questions seeking only one answer, or inquiries as to my personal, professional opinion based on my previous studies and experiences in the region. I was informed that they sought my personal opinion and that it was off the record! My response was that I honestly doubted if America would be allowed to stay in Uzbekistan once the airstrip and compound structures were completed and the Uzbekistanis gained the much-needed knowledge on how to operate the facility. When I was asked why I immediately responded that, I doubted if the Uzbekistan government was honestly interested in having a US military establishment sitting on their soil because the Uzbek people, who were Sunni Muslims, were known throughout the Middle East as being among the most devout Muslims in the Central Asia region and have a *very* close relationship with the Afghanistan Muslims. My personal opinion was that they were merely interested in having the American government pay for and build a functional airstrip and base for them. I continued by adding that yes it was a strategic and well-placed air hub for the American military, but it was also a perfectly placed and well-needed airstrip hub for the radical Islamic movement. I was very impressed by the commander and the participant's unanimous decision not to break for lunch but to continue straight through with the discussions and training. Obviously my personal opinion was not appreciated, nor was the fact that the commander chose to continue through lunch without a break by the air force officer in charge of the day's training secession, as he offered to go off the base to purchase lunch for everyone. However, when he returned to our session he had purchased lunch for all of the participants but not for me. He did not offer to go and purchase lunch for me so consequently I had to continue lecturing from 8 a.m. till after 4 p.m. with no breaks and with no lunch. This type of rudeness and lack of respect I endured from the time I was invited to lecture, my arrival and departure at the airport in Dayton, and during my lecture—not by the participants but by the air force staff who was in charge of the lecture. This type of conduct and disrespect I had not received during any of my previous years as an intelligence lecturer for DOD and the US military. I was correct in my prediction, as in August of 2005 the Uzbekistan government evicted the United States military from its well-made free air hub. Yes, I was ridiculed and blackballed because I wanted to learn the Arab/Islamic mind-set, culture, and Islamic sacred texts from "the horse's mouth," as my father always said, and because I had a keen insight that many chose to ignore and/or to deny. I was very genuine in my interest and in my respect for each individual who assisted me in understanding and developing a deep respect for them and their culture and faith. Not all Muslims are radical terrorists and not all terrorists are Arab/ Muslims. The twenty-first century radical Islamist is a universal movement with no boundaries, no one nationality, and no one race or gender. It is this extraordinarily devoted and deadly movement that the pages in this book reveal and discuss.

In chapter I, "The Revival of the Radical Islamic Movement," I describe the Muslim Brotherhood and how it has led a universal revival movement of Islam by calling for a global Jihad using a militia military force, a psychological battlefield, and by a global "Civilization Jihad" or infiltration. The words of the 500 BC war hero Sun Tzu best describe their strategy in the following quote: *"Oh, divine art of subtlety and secrecy! Through you we learn to be invisible, through you inaudible, and hence hold the enemy's fate in our hands."* **(1)** The roots of the Muslim Brotherhood are deeply engrained within al-Qaeda, ISIS, and the universal radical Islamic movement. In this chapter I explain how the oldest Muslim terrorist group, formed in 1928, has influenced and restored a powerful radical movement to *"eliminate and destroy the Western civilization from within and sabotage it by their own hands."* This act of eliminating and destroying the Western civilization is not only defined but described step-by-step in the Muslim Brotherhood document titled *"An Explanatory Memorandum on the General Strategic Goal for the Group in North America."* This document, along with numerous other evidence and testimonies, was used by the US government in the trial the US v the Holy Land Foundation, in which several leaders of the Muslim Brotherhood were tried and incarcerated. The motto for the Muslim Brotherhood movement is, **"Allah is our goal, the Messenger is our guide, the Qur'an is our law. Jihad is our way. Dying in the way of Allah is our highest aspiration."**

Chapter II, titled "The Soul of Islam: The Roots to the Bond of Brotherhood," reveals the sixteen key factors from the immigration of Muhammad, known in Islamic history as the night journey or *Hijrah*, from Mecca to Yathrib (Medina) in the year 622 AD, that changed the fate of Islam and is the motivation and role model that is dictating the present day radical Islamist movement. Each of these key factors dictates the mindset, the motivation, and the behavior and actions of the twenty-first century radical Islamic mujahidin (warrior). The *Hijrah* serves as the true bond between these warriors and Allah and Muhammad. It is during this period known as the Medina period in Muhammad's life that the fate of Islam is revealed and marked for all future generations. For it is during this period in the Prophet's life that he receives *"the sacred seal of the Prophet"* from Allah and he becomes not just the religious leader of his new converts but now he also becomes their legislator and their warrior leader. The seventh century Muhammad has become the role model for the twenty-first century radical Islamic mujahidin. Revising "the soul of Islam" to its original status as established by Muhammad after the Hijrah is the responsibility and obligation of all Muslims.

Chapter III describes how religion dictates the ideology of this revised version of the seventh century warrior, an ideology that has its roots in the Islamic historical error of the seventh century and the revelations received from Allah during Muhammad's life in Medina as recorded in the sacred texts of the Holy Qur'an and the Sunnah and Hadith (sayings and deeds of Muhammad). For the radical Islamist the world is divided into two geographical regions—the world of *"Dar-al-Islam"* (a world ruled by the Divine Laws of Allah known as Shari'ah law) or a world of *"Dar-al-Harb"* (a world of war or a world ruled by man-made laws and not the Divine Laws of Allah). According to their religious-based ideology, anyone who lives in the world of *"Dar-al-Harb"* is automatically recognized as an enemy of Islam. The ideology of the radical Islamic movement is an effort to control not only the reality among its followers but also the global Islamic *ummah* (community) and its sympathizers. Upon a precise researching of their ideology it became evident that their ideology actually establishes both their social identity and their self-identity. It is this dual identity that allows the new recruits to feel obligated to join the fight to "purify Islam," that "Islam is the victim," and it raises their expectations of their life in the hereafter ((*Akhirah*). By their acceptance and willingness to perform and be part of such horrendous acts of violence they have made themselves part of the Islamic historical battle for the "purification of the soul of Islam" in what has become a leaderless Global Jihad. The true significance of any ideology is that it must follow the fact that power is rarely exercised without some form of ideas and beliefs that justify their support and belief. In the minds of the radical Islamists they are "warriors of Allah's" and are obligated to establish one world under Islam. Why? Because **"Islam is the only religion in the sight of Allah." (2)**

For the radical Islamist, "Jihad" is an intrinsic part of Islam; therefore, their legitimacy and justification for all of their horrendous acts of violence are embedded in the sacred text of Islam. In chapter IV, "Fighting for the Soul of Islam: The Global Jihad," I elaborate on how Allah has not only made Jihad obligatory for all Muslims but also clearly defines who they are to fight and destroy, how they are to destroy them and their rewards for obeying and taking part in a Jihad as "warriors of Allah." I elaborate these factors by using numerous verses from Surat 9, "*At-Tawbah*," also known as "Chapter on War" and other Surat verses from the Holy Qur'an, which abrogates all previous Quranic verses given during Muhammad's life in Mecca, the period in his life before his night journey the Hijrah to Yathrib (Medina), in Saudi Arabia. For it was not until after this historical immigration that Muhammad became a religious, political, legislative, and military leader for his Islamic converts. There is a significant difference in the revelations Muhammad received during his persecution in Mecca, when he was a missionary seeking converts, to that of the revelations he received in Medina, when he was a warrior and a legislator establishing the first Islamic *ummah* (community). For example, in Surat 9, verse 5, also known as "the verse of the sword" abrogates about 100 or more verses that Muhammad received from Allah during his religious missionary life in Mecca. **For the radical Islamist, "Jihad" is the Sixth Pillar of Islam.**

In order for any nation to establish an effective counterterrorism strategy they must have a conclusive and extensive understanding of not only who their enemy is but also the "battlefield" on which they have chosen to fight. The "battlefield" the radical Islamists have declared and are using so effectively is public manipulation and deception, known as psychological warfare. They are using propaganda, threats, and other psychological techniques to mislead, intimidate, demoralize, or otherwise influence the thinking and behavior of their opponents' government and citizens. Chapter V, "The Twenty-First Century Battlefield" reveals how every international media release has been well staged and strategically directed as part of their intimidation and demoralization of their chosen targeted enemy. They have used and published staged military militia and horrendous acts of brutality and their unique and strategically organized *"Civilization Jihad Settlements"* to inflict fear and intimidation. Their **"Civilization Jihad Settlement Process"** is strategically defined step-by-step in the confiscated memorandum of the Muslim Brotherhood and was used as evidence in the US v

Holy Land Foundation trial. It is a "process for eliminating by their <u>own hands.</u>" **(3)** Propaganda warfare has been taken to a new level in the twenty-first century under the leadership of the Muslim Brotherhood and incorporated into the radical Islamic movement.

Chapter VI, the conclusion, makes a concerted effort to answer four very distinguishable questions asked not only by Americans but also by governments and citizens throughout the world. Why have they targeted America? What do they want? Why homegrown terrorists? Why are they targeting and killing innocent citizens? Jihad may be waged against injustice or an unjust nation, as Islam defines the terms. For the radical Islamist the world is divided into two very clearly defined areas only: (1) the world of *"Dar-al-Islam"* or the land of Islam and (2) the land of *"Dar-al-Harb"* or the land of war and injustice. For the radical Islamist, Islam is justice and no-Islam is injustice. As a major world player and a nation founded on the separation of state and religion, America was destined to become a major target for the radical Islamist movement. The radical Islamists believe that **when** they conquer America and force its citizens and government to be ruled only by Shari'ah law that there will be a domino effect among other world players, whether they be Muslim or non-Muslim. Therefore, according to Islamic law, a "just war" can be waged against a nation or people who do not submit to Islam. What do they want? Their answer to this question is very clear and has been stated many times by its leaders, scholars and mujahidin. For the radical Islamist, Islam is not a religion merely seeking a declaration of the freedom of the Arabs nor is its message confined merely to Muslims. For Islam addresses the whole of mankind, and its sphere of work is the whole earth. God is the Sustainer, not merely of the

Arabs, nor is His providence limited to those who believe in the faith of Islam, for God is the Sustainer of the creator of the whole world. Radical leaders have taken bits and pieces from the sacred sayings of the Prophet, peace be upon him, and used them to influence and motivate their recruits. For example: "The earth has been made for me (and for my followers)." However the rest of that quotes states, "a place for praying and a thing to perform *Tayammum*, thereafter anyone of my followers can pray wherever the time of a prayer is due. Every Prophet used to be sent to his nation only but I have been sent to all mankind." **(4)** The twenty-first century radical Islamist movement is on a mission to return the (whole) world to its Sustainer and Creator and free it from servitude to anyone other than Allah. In the sight of Islam, anyone who serves and follows laws devised by man and not by Allah is outside of God's religion and therefore an abomination to God. Which answers the question, "Why are they targeting and killing innocent citizens?" Their motivation and goal is the creation of a universal *"Dar-al-Islam"* which means creating a world solely ruled by Shari'ah law and making all of its inhabitants devoted to and submitted exclusively to Allah and the Divine Laws. Any citizen who pays taxes, attends schools and universities, supports the military, and accepts money and services from a non-Muslim ruling government automatically is guilty of living in the world of *"Dar-al-Harb"* and therefore a prime target. As chapter VI reveals, their targeting and killing of innocent citizens has become a powerful and influential recruiting tool.

Four major historical events occurred in 1979 in the Middle East that served as warnings that a revival was in the making within the radical Islamic movement. The **first** event was the overthrow of the Shah Mohammad Reza Pahlavi's leadership in Iran, headed by the Ayatollah Ruhollah Khomeini, and the hostage-taking of American diplomats by force and by a group of Iranian citizens. The radical Islamists claimed that it was the first true Islamic theocracy to be installed in over five century's time. With this one act of violence and the taking of hostages by the citizens of Iran, terrorism took a new turn and became an act of violence against a sovereign nation by a non-sovereign Islamic movement. The **second** major incident that shattered the Islamic world in 1979 was the attack and seizure of the Grand Mosque in Mecca by a group of Islamic radicals who demanded that the Saudi Arabian government prove its legitimacy as a Muslim ruling nation. The Muslim media reported that the Mosque had been seized by Americans, which caused international bloodshed and hatred of Americans. It was soon reported by the Saudi Arabian government that it was not Americans but rather Iranians who had seized the Grand Mosque, but the propaganda was already on the streets and in the minds of young Muslims. The **third** historical event was in Afghanistan, a war between the Soviet Union and the citizens of Afghanistan. It was from this war that the first call was made for young Muslims throughout the world to form a universal brotherhood and come to Afghanistan to defend their brother Muslims and the Islamic ummah. It was from this young brotherhood of fighters that al-Qaeda was formed and the first non-national movement was born. The **fourth** major event that rocked the Middle East and the Muslim world was the signing of the Camp David Agreement in 1979 between Israel and Egypt. This agreement caused enormous controversy within the Muslim and Arab world, and Egypt was suspended from the Arab League in 1979 until 1989. President Sadat of Egypt was assassinated on October 6, 1981, because of this agreement by members of his own military, who were also members of the

Muslim Brotherhood terrorist organization. What made these four events so catastrophic for the international community was the global awakening of the radical Islamists' desires to establish the return of the "Soul of Islam" as created and established under the leadership of the Prophet Muhammad and directed by the revelations of Allah. It is only by affirming their bond of brotherhood that the revival for the purification of Islam can be effective.

Of the many audiences I had in mind when writing this book, it is primarily for intelligence studies of the radical Islamic movement, professionals, additional text for graduate school courses on terrorism and counterterrorism, homeland security and national security, students and government analysts, and interested public readers. Many books have been written about the organizations of the radical Islamic movement and their history, their brutality, and their propaganda, but I have not been able to find books which actually define how they have been radicalized and what their actual driving force is. It was my desire and commitment to provide a book that offered a new insight into the radical Islamic roots and its revival, for I believe that unless we have an educated and intelligent concept of just how these young individuals from around the world actually think and what their driving ideology is then we are fighting a losing battle. The twenty-first century radical Islamist movement claims that "the world is at war with Islam."

A few very important factors to be noted: (1) Throughout this book the Arabic word *Allah* signifies the word God; (2) the Arabic word *ummah* signifies the universal Muslim community; (3) the Arabic word *mujahid* refers to all Muslims who fight in the way of Allah (Mujahidin is plural); (4) the Arabic word *Sunna* (also spelt *Sunnah)* is the traditional part of Islamic law and is virtually the words and sayings of the Prophet Muhammad and recorded within the sacred text of the Hadith (throughout this book I have used the spelling *Sunnah* so that it will not be confused with the Arabic word *Sunni, the name of the* largest Islamic religious sect). (5) all references to the Revelations of Allah are taken from the Holy Qur'an published by the King Fahd Holy , Qur'an Printing Complex in Mecca, Saudi Arabia, and all quotes are marked in the following format (9:10) meaning Surat 9 verse 10 of the Holy Qur'an; (6) all quotes referenced to the Qur'an and/or the Bible are in bold print in order to distinguish them from other quotes; (7) in Islam the branch of worshipers known as "Shia" rejects the first three Caliphs and regards Ali, the forth Caliph, as the true successor to Muhammad (the Shia worshipers are called Shiite); and (8) to emphasis the importance of a statement that is paramount in answering the questions as to who and why of the radical Islamist movement I have noted in bold print.

NOTES

1. Sun Tzu, *The Art of War*, Chartwell Books, 2012

2. The Holy Qur'an, Surat 3:19

3. "An Explanatory Memorandum on the General Strategic Goal for the Group in North America," Government Exhibit 003-0085 3:04-CR-240-G.

4. Sahih al-Bukhari Hadith Book 7, #336, narrated Jabir bin 'Abdullah. http://al-islamic.net/hadith/bukhari/7. (Retrieved 11/21/2017)

I
THE REVIVAL OF THE RADICAL ISLAMIST MOVEMENT: THE MUSLIM BROTHERHOOD

Allah is our goal, the Messenger is our guide, The Qur'an is our law. Jihad is our way. Dying in the way of Allah is our highest aspiration."

—Motto of the Muslim Brotherhood

"Civilization Jihad Settlement Process for eliminating and destroying the Western civilization from within and 'sabotaging' its miserable house <u>by their own hands.</u>" (1)

The birth of the largest and oldest Islamic terrorist movement can be traced to the country of Egypt following the end of WWI.

It was formed because of (1) the fall of the Ottoman Islamic Empire, (2) the abolishment of the Islamic Caliphate, (3) the presence of and rule of Great Britain and (4) the Western super powers under the League of Nations mandates of the Arab region. The Egyptian-based Sunni radical Islamist movement is called the Muslim Brotherhood (MB) or *Ikhwan,* and is the initiator and the facilitator of the most brutal and vengeful radical terrorist organizations in the world. **The MB and its radical Islamic network hold literalistic views of the Qur'an, the Hadith, the Sunnah, and Shari'ah law.** The Egyptian based MB has various active known terrorist organizations under its umbrella such as *Hamas* (the Arabic acronym for *The Islamic Resistance Movement (Harakat al-Muqawamah al-Islamiyya)* **(2),** and **(3)** *al-Qaeda* (the Base), the *Islamic State of Iraq and Syria* (ISIS and/or ISIL), the *Muslim Brotherhood of Syria* (MBS), the *Palestine Islamic Jihad* (PIJ), the *Palestine Liberation Organization* (PLO), the *Palestine Muslim Brotherhood,* the *Al-Islah* in Yemen, the *Pakistan Muslim Brotherhood,* the *Reform Movement of Somalia,* and numerous other worldwide terrorist networks. The MB is the best organized, has the most effective infiltration system, and is the most powerful transnational terrorist network in the world. Its English website, *Ikhwanweb,* describes the organization's principles and objective that Shari'ah law "is the basis for controlling the affairs of state and society." Found within MB's bylaws, Article 2 (A) clearly defines that: "the Muslim Brotherhood is an international Muslim Body which seeks to establish Allah's law in the land by achieving the spiritual goals of Islam and the true religion" and "the need to inform the masses, Muslims and non-Muslims, of Islamic teachings, explaining the signs in detail to those who understand the pure human nature upon which Allah Has created man." How they will achieve this objective and vision of informing the masses that Islam is the true religion for the world is defined in Article 3, section (A) "Preaching to Islam, this can only be achieved by promoting it through various means such as radio and television, pamphlets, bulletins, newspapers, magazines, books, publications and preparing the delegation and missions at home and abroad"; and section (D) describes MB's game plan for infiltrating a *Dar-al-Harb* nation: "Make every effort for the establishment of educational, social, economic, and scientific institutions and the establishment of mosques, schools, clinics, shelters, clubs, as well as the formation of communities to regulate zakat affairs and alms". Also clearly defined within section E is that it is the duty and the responsibility of every Muslim to join the global Jihad against all infidels in Allah's cause in establishing a universal Islamic ummah: **"Islamic nation must be fully prepared to fight the tyrants and the enemies of Allah as a prelude to establishing an Islamic state."** **(4)** It is the objectives and principles found within the by-laws of the MB that has become a major part of the radical Islamist global Jihad movement.

In 2017 the Muslim Brotherhood movement is estimated to have either actively affiliated terrorist groups and/or actively working cells in almost every nation in the world including America, all the Western European nations and Africa and Asia. Their motto, or their credo as they refer to it, is "God is our objective, the Qur'an is our Constitution, the Prophet is our leader, struggle [Jihad] is our way, and death for the sake of God is the highest of our aspirations." This exemplifies their objective (**Warriors of God**), purpose (**Jihad/war**), and their blueprint as defined in the **Holy Qur'an** and in the words and deeds of Muhammad—the **Sunnah/Hadith**. Its international supremacy and expansion of its ideology is due to its hierarchal organizational structure starting at the top with the Shura Council responsible for establishing and charting the policies and strategies of the global organization. Next in line in their organizational hierarchy is the Executive Office, also known as the Guidance Office, which consists of the MB members who are leaders of each division of the organization. Members of the Executive Office are elected to their post by the Shura Council which also directs and controls their leadership and policies. It is in this hierarchal structure and the ideology and literary teachings of two very important and influential men—Sheikh Hassan al-Banna and Al-Shaheed Sayyid Qutb—that the Muslim Brotherhood blueprint and motivation for the present-day twenty-first century, radical terrorist strategies and movement can be found.

The Muslim Brotherhood's literalistic views of the Qur'an, the Hadith, the Sunnah and Shari'ah law can be traced to its founder, a humble Egyptian scholar, school teacher, and Imam by the name of Sheikh Hassan al-Banna, who formed the Sunni religious-based organization known as the Society of Muslim Brothers in 1928 (1347AH). This newly established movement opposed the power and brutality of the Western colonization and the lack of Islamic religious morals and values found within the Muslim ummah following WWI. Like Saddam Hussein, the former dictator of Iraq, Al-Banna was a devout admirer of Adolf Hitler and his cleansing for a "pure race." (Confiscated documents taken from Hitler's bunkers following WWII revealed that a large number of MB members served in the Nazi Schutzstaffel (SS) militancy protective police force.) It is interesting to note that the MB militancy and covert force that was formed under and during Hitler's regime is still found today, called the "Special Chapter" of the MB operations. History has shown that the violent and aggressive actions of members of the MB during and after WWII were all based on their objective of enforcing a strict Shari'ah law—the Divine Law of Allah. Al-Banna's objective was to legitimize Islam and to return Islam to its original religious/political roots as formed by the Prophet Muhammad and the first four Caliphs. This blueprint, not only for the Muslim Brotherhood but also today's twenty-first century radical Islamist movements, can be found in al-Banna's book titled *Jihad,* which has become a powerful recruiting tool and motivator for young radical Muslims throughout the world. Echoing the prophet Muhammad's Sunnah, al-Banna expressed in his book that, "Jihad is an obligation from Allah on every Muslim and cannot be ignored or evaded," and, "Furthermore Allah has specifically honored the mujahidin with certain exceptional qualities both spiritual and practical to benefit them in this world and the next." **(5)** The most famous of al-Banna's ideology and literary rhetoric is still echoed around the world by Islamic scholars and leaders: **"It is the nature of Islam to dominate, not to be dominated, to impose its law on all nations and to extend its power to the entire planet."** **(6)** If one were to read the Salafi mission and its objectives and justification to justify violent action one would note the duplication of al-Banna's objectives. There is one objective stressed by al-Banna that was not found within the original Salafi mission and that is that all Western ideas must be banned from the Muslim ummah. It is because of al-Banna's determination and dedication between the 1930s and the 1940s to establish an Islamist movement that would: (1) regain its status in the world; (2) destroy any Jewish state; (3) return its true identity as established by Muhammad; (4) reestablish its loyalty to the solidarity of a universal Muslim ummah (community); and (5) enforce *"hudud"* as the most serious of crimes and demanding severe divine punishment as mandated under Shari'ah law. Al-Banna was disheartened by the present Islamic status in the world prior to and after WWI. The Islamic ummah from 632 AD to the eleventh century were the rulers in the world of intellectual scholars, scientific and medical technology, and cross-cultural advancement known as the "Islamic Golden Age." While the Islamic Empire was enjoying their Golden Age, Europe was in its "Dark Ages." Starting in the end of the tenth century, Islam fell from its prominent status due to the influence and direction of its Islamic scholars and Imams who rejected any form of intellectual and/or critical thinking and demanded blind obedience to (1) the Holy Qur'an, (2) the saying and deeds of the Prophet Muhammad and (3) the Divine Laws of Allah. WWI revealed just how backward and underdeveloped the Arab/Islamic world had become, which in turn caused great humiliation and shame to the global Islamic ummah. Someone had to take the blame for this humiliation and shame and al-Banna was positive that the extent of corruption in the Islamic ummah was directly caused by the invasion of the Western secular principles, morals, and technical advancement. However, if one studies Islamic history, one learns that this falling from prominence occurred centuries before WWI and was caused by the Islamic religious leaders' rejection of all forms of intellectual thinking and technology. This is supposedly "when the global Muslim ummah fell out of Allah's grace," as one elderly Islamic scholar informed me. I immediately searched my Qur'an to find the basis for his claim and found in Surat 8:46 Allah's very clear instructions that all true followers of Islam are to be: **"content not with one another, so that you become weak and your strength departs, and persevere, for Allah is with those who persevere."** The Islamic religious leaders banned all contacts and cross-intellectual advancements of Western European and Asian ideas and thereby reversed the intellectual and technical advancements and knowledge that the world had known and experienced from the Islamic world during its superior reign—the Islamic Golden Age. Islam had been the intellectual leader in science, astronomy, economics, medical advancements, and literary and scholarly materials prior to their religious leaders banning any form of intellectual and physical contact with the outside world. Blind obedience was strictly enforced during this back period in Islamic history. Al-Banna believed that Allah had "ordained the Muslim Brotherhood as the enforcer of Shari'ah law for all mankind." It was during his reign as leader of the MB that the organization launched a pro-Palestine campaign and took an active part in the 1935-1939 Arab revolt in Palestine. At the time of the crackdown and numerous arrests, which included their leader and founder al-Banna, in November of 1948 the brotherhood was estimated by the Egyptian government to have over 500,000 members and to be a terrorist organization. In 1949 the MB assassination of the Egyptian Prime Minister Nuqrashi Pasha led to the assassination of its leader, al-Banna, which in turn triggered a rise in the brutality and aggression of the MB in retaliation. Al-Banna's dedication and his extreme faith and vision for the return of the global Islamic ummah dominated not only the Muslim Brotherhood network but the entire global Islamic ummah. Al-Banna stressed that the only way to restore Islam's status and remove its humiliation and shame was by "mobilize [ing] the entire Ummah into one body to defend the right cause with all its strength . . . to Jihad, to warfare." (7)—a Global Jihad (war). The radical Islamist militia's movement believes that the Islamic revolt in the twenty-first century is the result of the (man-made) decisions following WWI—the Sykes Picot Agreement, the League of Nations Mandates, and failure of the Western Nations to accept and support the Arab/Islamic leaders in the region.

In 1952 and 1953 Egypt experienced a military coup staged by Colonel Gamel Abdal Nasser that deposed the monarchy of King Farouk and led the Muslim Brotherhood split and the formation of two branches. One branch worked with Colonel Nasser in forming a secular government but the second branch became a radical advocate movement. It was the second branch, under the leadership of Al-Shaheed Sayyid Qutb, a famous Egyptian Islamic theorist, poet, and author, of at least twenty-four books, that the Muslim Brotherhood became hostile against Nasser's secular government, and the various ruling Middle East monarchy regimes and against the decay in the moral and social values of the Islamic ummah. It was in Qutb's last book and his most famous literary work titled **Milestones** (Ma'alim fi al-T of ariq) that he divided the world into two entities—**Dar-al-Islam**, the land of Islam, and **Dar-al-Harb**, the land of war (nonbelievers)—**good versus evil**:

> **Only one place on earth can be called the home of Islam (*Dar-al-Islam*), and that is the place where the Islamic state is established and the Shari'ah is enforced and Allah's limits are observed and where all the Muslims administer the affairs of the community with mutual consultation.** The rest of the world is the home of hostility (*Dar-al-Harb*). A Muslim can have only two possible relations with *Dar-al-Harb*: peace with a contractual agreement, or war. **A country with which Muslims may have a treaty is not regarded as the home of Islam"** (8).

It is this clear division in the world between good versus evil that has become the cornerstone and motivation for the brutal and inhumane acts of violence plaguing the world today. This one quote also clearly divines the radical Islamist blueprint for why they have such profound hostility toward America, the Western European nations and any nation which they have designated as being evil (not a true Muslim nation controlled and dictated to by Shari'ah law). The last sentence in the above quote is the real power point in understanding any negotiating and/or treaty and agreements made between a non-Muslim nation and a Muslim nation. **"A country with which Muslims may have a treaty is not regarded as the home of Islam"** is based on the private ten-year peace treaty Muhammad agreed upon with the Quraysh tribe of Mecca in March of 628AD, known as the Treaty of Hudaybiyyah. However, in spite of the agreed ten-year duration period of the peace treaty Muhammad continued to invade the Quraysh trade caravans, conquer their territories and their water wells, and in 632AD he invaded and took control of their city, Mecca. Just because a non-Islamic nation has a treaty and/or agreement with an Islamic nation, for example the America/Iran Nuclear agreement of 2015, it does not automatically signify peace between the two nations or that the Islamic nation considers them to now be in the land of good, *Dar-al-Islam*, and that the Muslim nation has to honor the treaty. That is wishful thinking and very naive. In Qutb's following quote we learn that Muhammad was justified in not honoring the peace treaty because the Quraysh tribe was not following Shari'ah law and therefore they were automatically in the "home of Hostility *(Dar-al-Harb)*":

> But any place where the Islamic nation Shari'ah is not enforced and where Islam is not dominant becomes the home of Hostility (*Dar-al-Harb*). A Muslim will remain prepared to fight against it, whether it be his birthplace or a place where

his relatives reside or where his property or any other material interest are located. And thus Muhammad (peace be upon him) fought against the city of Mecca, although it was his birthplace, and his relatives lived there, and he and his companions had houses and property that they had left when they migrated, yet the soil of Mecca did not become *Dar-al-Islam* for him and his followers until it surrendered to Islam and the Shari'ah became operative in it. **(9)**

The United States of America is not a nation governed under Shari'ah law; therefore, it cannot be considered to be in the land of *Dar-al-Islam*. In lieu of this well-established and documented mind-set, not only found within the text of Qutb's famous literary work *Milestones* but also found in the Qur'an and Shari'ah law, I ask you one simple question: what is the true and honest legality of the 2015 American/Iran Nuclear Agreement? May I suggest that one take the time to Google and read the full document titled "Parameters for a Joint Comprehension Plan of Action Regarding the Islamic Republic of Iran's Nuclear Program"?

Nasser during his rule as President of Egypt from 1956 till his death in 1970 held numerous crackdowns and incarcerations of the MB organization members. Following his death in September of 1970 Muhammad Anwar Sadat became Nasser's successor and remained Egypt's president until his assassination on October 6, 1981, during Egypt's annual Victory Parade. During his presidency Sadat regained Egypt's ownership of the Sinai Peninsula in the Six Day war of 1967 and became an instant international hero for Egypt and the global Islamic ummah.

However, because of his involvement in the Camp David talks and his signing of the Egypt-Israel Peace Treaty in 1979, members of the MB and the radical Islamist movement believed him to be a traitor to both Arabs and Muslims. Although this was a marked historical incident and one that won both Sadat, as the first Arab in history, and Prime Minister Menachem Begin the Nobel Peace Prize, it infuriated many Arab and Muslim individuals. As Egypt's president, Sadat had lifted the various restrictions on the Brotherhood and released many of its imprisoned members, but because of this one act in defiance in the ideology of al-Banna and Qutb, members of the MB, who were also members of Egypt's military, assassinated Sadat. Following Sadat's assassination the MB experienced freedom of movement and growth till the 2011 Egyptian Revolution. By 2007 the MB had become very aggressive, won several seats in parliament and demanded that an Islamic cleric be appointed as overseer of the Egyptian government. Under President Muhammad Hosni Said Mubarak, Sadat's successor, who served as Egypt's President from 1981 till his forced resignation in 2011, he constantly was at battle with the MB movement opposition to his rule.

The MB transnational radical Islamist network has incorporated Qutb's ideology that the world is divided into *Dar-al-Islam* (good) and/or *Dar-al-Harb* (any land that is not under Shari'ah law) to judge and execute both Muslims and non-Muslims throughout the world. Following Qutb's instructions the MB set out to delegitimize any nation that was not ruled by their interpretation of strict Islamic Divine Law. Article 2 of the MB bylaws introduction states: "The Muslim Brotherhood is an international Muslim Body, which seeks to establish Allah's law in the land by achieving the spiritual goals of Islam and the true religion by the following means." Section E in Article 2 defines one of those "means" as "Insist to liberate the Islamic nation from the yoke of foreign rule, help safeguard the rights of Muslims everywhere and unite Muslims around the world." **(10)** Two examples of the significance of the bylaw being actively used by the MB and the radical Islamist movement would be (1) bin Laden's rhetoric published as a threat against the Saudi Arabian Royal Family and his al-Qaeda's guerilla attacks against the monarchy of Saudi Arabia because, as he claimed, their friendship with America made them *Dar-al-Harb*, or the land of war, and (2) the MB 2011 'Arab Spring' that swept across the Middle East Arab nations and changed the ruling infrastructure of the region. The 'Arab Spring,' also called the 'Arab Awakening' and/or the 'Arab Spring and Winter,' was a well-organized and implemented series of civil wars and riots that began as the Tunisian Revolution in December of 2010 and soon spread to include all of the Arab League nations. Qutb believed that "the whole world is steeped in *Jahiliyyah*" **(11),** "*Jahiliyyah* is evil and corrupt, whether it be of the ancient or modern variety" **(12),** and therefore, "we must free ourselves from the clutches of *jahili* society, *jahili* concepts, *jahili* traditions, and *jahili* leadership" **(13)**. By February of 2012 the rulers of Tunisia, Iraq, Egypt, Libya, and Yemen were forced out of power and were replaced by members of the radical Islamist movement. One historical and noteworthy change made by the MB in the 2011 revolts was the fall of the Hosni Mubarak presidency and party in Egypt and the establishment of a self-declared member who ran for election representing the Muslim Brotherhood: Mohamed Morsi. He was a recognized and supported candidate of a sovereign Arab nation by the United States president Barack Obama. But within a year of his election as President of Egypt, Morsi had enforced strict Shari'ah law, had appointment himself as having power over all legislative and judicial acts, and established a referendum to the Egyptian constitution in reference to journalists, non-violent demonstrators, military trials, and detention without a judicial review for up to thirty days. Morsi's and the Muslim Brotherhoods' enforcement of strict Shari'ah law and their dictatorship over the government, military, and citizens of Egypt led to an enormous crackdown on their movement and the arrest and overthrow of their new government by the Egyptian military in July of 2013. Mohamed Morsi was sentenced to death on the sixteenth of May, 2015, along with over a hundred MB members. The initial civil wars dictated in Qutb's *Milestones* and acted out by the MB and radical Islamists in the 'Arab Spring' is still being fought in both the countries of Syria and Iraq. This ideology is clearly noted in the following quote of Sayyid Qutb: "In the world there is only one party of Allah; all others are parties of Satan and rebellion." **(14)** It is very important that the reader fully comprehends how deeply rooted the radical Islamist ideology and their blueprints are in Sayyid Qutb's belief that the world can only be divided into two entities: "good versus evil" - there is no in-between or maybe. It is "either-or -only" for the MB and the radical Islamist movement. For the Muslim Brotherhood, they are obligated and justified to enforce Qutb's ideology because al-Banna, their founder, deemed that it was Allah who authorized the MB to be His superior enforcers of the Divine Law. **The real key factor to comprehend is that it doesn't actually matter what the people believe or even what they may actually have faith in, but what really matters in Shari'ah law is HOW the people behave and act upon their beliefs and faith.** Qutb, in his book *Milestones,* made it very clear that **"Islam is the real civilization"** in the world **(15).** This ideology is supported by Allah's revelation found in Surat 16:90: **"commands justice, like doing of good, and giving to kith and kin, and He forbids all indecent deeds, and evil and rebellion:**

He instructs you, that ye may receive admonition." For Qutb all devout Muslims are required to avoid everything and anything that can be recognized as being shameful, immoral, and/or any inward rebellion or evilness against Allah, **His Divine laws,** and His last Prophet Muhammad. For Qutb, an ummah that lived by the pure Islamic values found within the sacred text of the Holy Qur'an, the Sunnah, the Hadith, and the Divine laws of Allah (Shari'ah laws) was the only pure global Islamic ummah.

Upon his return from America in 1951 he joined the Egyptian MB and soon replaced al-Banna as their intellectual and theological leader throughout the 1950s and 60s. It is his famous literary rhetoric known as *Qutbism* that has enabled the Muslim Brotherhood to become the largest and most influential militancy mind set of the global radical Islamist movement. He proclaimed that the nature of Islam was to rule the world, as set forth by Allah and proclaimed by His last prophet Muhammad, and that they were authorized to use *"whatever resources were available."* Qutb stressed that a *"pure"* global Islamic ummah must be patterned after that established by Muhammad in the early years of Islam. Muhammad, upon his immigration to Medina, sought to establish a pure Islamic ummah free from all the impurities found in the world around him. The twenty-first century radical Islamist followers of the *Qutbism* ideology believe that the Qur'an dictates and authorizes their aggression, brutality and revenge with *"whatever resources were available."* ***"But do not give the fools property that Allah assigned to you"*** *(Surat 4:4)*. Qutb advocated that the Jihadist must first establish one country as a *Dar-al-Islam* to establish a world presence— hence al-Qaeda's failed effort to claim Afghanistan and/or Pakistan as the new Islamic *Dar-al-Isla*m countries, and in 2015, ISIS took over and claimed that Iraq was the new Islamic *Dar* *al-Islam* by establishing the second major presences required in Islam—the new caliphate. Qutb advocated that the only way to establish a world of Muslim purity, **Dar al-Islam**, was by revolutionary fury of Allah against the land of war, **Dar- al-Harb.**

It was during the mid-1950s and because of Nasser's rule and crackdown on the Muslim Brotherhood's movements in Egypt that many of its members sought refuge as professors and professional leaders in various Arab and European nations and in the United States. Many of these new Muslim Brotherhood Sunni immigrants, refugees, and former professors and/or scholars were graduates and/or professors at the oldest (founded in 970 AD) chief Arabic and Islamic Law University in the world, Al-Azhar University, located in Egypt. As graduates and professors of the Cairo al-Azhar University, named after the Prophet Muhammad's daughter Fatimah who was also known as "al-Zahra" or the luminous one, these Muslim Brotherhood radical intellectuals filled the void in nations like Saudi Arabia, Kuwait, Pakistan, Afghanistan, Syria, Yemen, and the Western European and American universities. Two very prominent MB intellectuals who left a legacy in the twenty-first century radical Islamist movement can be traced to the King Abdul Aziz University in Jeddah, were Muhammad Qutb, brother of the famous leader and theorist of the ideology Sayyid Qutb, and Abdullah Yusuf Azzam, known as the *"godfather of Global Jihad"* and cofounder of al-Qaeda and the Maktab al-Khidamat. Both of these men believed in and taught the strict ideology of al-Banna and Sayyid Qutb to the future generations of radical Islamist mujahidin , such as the Saudi-born Usama bin Laden (the late leader and cofounder of Al-Qaeda); the Egyptian doctor Ayman Mohammed Rabie al-Zawahiri (current leader of al-Qaeda); Yasser Arafat (former founder and leader of the

PLO); Pakistani Ramzi Ahmed Yousef (1993 WTC bomber) and his uncle Khalid Shaikh Mohammed (the mastermind behind the 9/11 attacks and a graduate of North Carolina Agricultural and Technical State University); Sheikh Omar Abdel Rahman, also known as the Islamic blind Imam who preached Jihad from the pulpit in the Mosque in Brooklyn and called for a Holy War (Jihad) against America (Rahman was found guilty for his part in the initial planning of the 1993 WTC bombing); and Saudi Arabian Mohammed Jamal Khalifa (bin Laden's brother-in-law who was arrested in Lebanon and in Jordan for various terrorist bombings and for his involvements in filtering money to al-Qaeda), just to name a few.

By the 1960s and 1970s, many of the Afghan religious scholars had been influenced by the teachings of Muhammad Qutb and/or Abdulla Azzam. Qutb's ideas attracted particular interest in the faculty of the religious law department at Kabul University. One such individual was Professor Burhanuddin Rabbani, who received a degree in Islamic Law and theology from Kabul University and a master's degree in Islamic Philosophy from Cairo al-Azhar University in 1968. Rabbani, whose instructors at both universities were both scholars and advocates of the Muslim Brotherhood ideology, was influenced by the teachings and literary writings of both al-Banna and Sayyid Qutb. As an active mujahidin during the Soviet occupation of Afghanistan and as the leader of the MB activist movement, *"the Jamiat-e-Islami"* also known as *"the Islamic Society"* (a documented active radical Islamist terrorist movement that promoted fundamentalism and enforced strict Shari'ah law), Rabbani went on to serve as the official president of Afghanistan from 1992 until the Taliban takeover in 1996. He was assassinated on September 20, 2011, in Kabul, Afghanistan.

It was also during this same period, the 1950s that many scholars and intellectuals of the Muslim Brotherhood immigrated and became infiltrated into the American infrastructure. On September 23, 1953, al-Banna's son-in-law and close fellow associate Sa'id Ramadan was part of a delegation of Muslim Brotherhood members who had a private meeting in the White House Oval Office with President Dwight D. Eisenhower **(16)**. This meeting, according to various historical records, occurred because of the Muslim Brotherhood's close relationship with Adolf Hitler's anti-Semitic movement in WWII and because many of its members had joined Hitler's SS and Brown Shirt police squads. Evidently it was this close relationship with Hitler that allowed the Brotherhood to move easily into the European nations and establish numerous fixed branches that are still in existence and very active today. Unfortunately the American government and her allies were easily persuaded by the Muslim Brotherhood clandestine operatives that they would help them in developing and enforcing their strategic Cold War plans against the atheist Soviet Union—an **excellent example of the old Arab proverb "*The enemy of my enemy is my friend to help me get rid of my enemy but they are still my enemy.*"** And an excellent example of the effectiveness of this old proverb would be how Abdullah Yusuf Azzam and other radical Islamists sought the financial and physical aid of the United States (enemy of their enemy) to help them fight (against their enemy) the Soviet Union in Afghanistan (who was also the enemy of the Soviet Union during the Cold War era) and following their victory (the Muslims) turned on their enemy (the United States). The very nation that they had sought financial and military assistance from in their fight to defeat the Soviet Union was still their enemy. An important factor in this proverb is that the United States was locked into the 'Cold War' with the

Soviet Union and it was a perfect enemy to latch onto to help the Muslims as both the US and the Arab/Muslim world were at war against the Soviet Union.

The prime strategies of the Muslim Brotherhood to sabotage and infiltrate the infrastructures and the establishments and to create a strong political and religious presence within the educational, technical, business, social, and political foundations of America can be found in four well-planned and defined blueprints. The **first** blueprint was, composed in 1928 and posted in 2005 on the MB-established English website, www.*ikwanweb*, was the organizations bylaws. Part I of said bylaws consists of six chapters and fifty-four articles that clearly define their "objectives" and their "how-to strategies" to accomplish these objectives. The MB *bylaws* are so significant in understanding their strategies and mind-set that I have duplicated some of the material in this chapter and feel there is a need to go even deeper into the power and influence that these bylaws have on the radical Islamist twenty-first century movement. Chapter II of Part I, titled "Objectives and Means," clearly defined the MB as "an international Muslim Body," whose main goal and purpose is "to establish Allah's law (Divine Law or Shari'ah law) in the land." In Article (2) of chapter II we learn that it is the duty of all members of the MB to "inform the masses, Muslim and non-Muslim, of Islamic teachings" (Section A); and that as members they must "**endeavor to purify the hearts and souls of men from evil and sin** (Section B); but they must also as members **"work on establishing the Islamic State and defend the nation against the internal enemies (evil, infidels, and/or non-believers)** (Section E). This strategy, in order to work, must have "the sincere support for a global cooperation in accordance with the provision of Islamic Shari'ah. . . and active participation toward building a new basis of human civilization as it is ensured by the overall teachings of Islam."(Section G) of Chapter II is calling on all Muslims throughout the world, the Universal (Global) Ummah, to participate in this blueprint of the Muslim Brotherhood—hence the homegrown terrorist and no race or nationality significance **(17)**. It is important to stress here that in Islam there can be no nationality loyalty for loyalty belongs to Allah and to Allah only. Continuing in the significance of the MB bylaws Article 3, of Chapter II defines the various strategies which the Brotherhood will use **"in achieving these objectives"** starting with (Section A) **"promoting Islam through various means such as radio and television, pamphlets, newspapers, magazines, books, publications and preparing the delegation and missions at home and abroad." The radical Islamists have mastered propaganda using Adolph Hitler's strategies and style**. (Section B) "Teach the movement's (MB) younger members to flourish with these principles and demonstrate the true meaning of religiousness as individuals and families." This *"objective"* is totally meant in the twenty-first century by the MB organizations that fall under its umbrella, such as the *Muslim Student Organization,* very similar to Hitler's youth organizations and policies. (Section C) of Article 3 of Chapter II provides guidance and a blueprint which is a sound approach suitable for Muslims in the fields of education, legislation, judiciary, administration, military life, economy, health and governance: "This may be aimed at by presenting thorny issues to the competent authorities in order to persuade the world's legislative and executive bodies to follow through with the original conceptual thinking and the tactical implementation with the necessity to work hard to refine the media guided by Islam" and is continued in (Section D) in which the MB members are to "Make every effort for the establishment of educational, social, economic and scientific institutions and the establishment of mosques, schools, clinics, shelters, clubs as well as the formation of committees to regulate zakat affairs and alms. Seeking to bring reconciliation between Allah, individuals, families, and resist succumbing to social ills, harmful habits, drugs, alcohol, gambling by guiding young people to the right path filling their leisure time with positive activities by creating independent sections in accordance with special regulations." Please reread Section D several times as it clearly defines what America is facing today (twenty-first century) in the infiltration and sabotaging of its infrastructure and policies. (Section E) of Article 3, Chapter II in the bylaws clearly defines for the international ummah and the international MB members that **"The Islamic nation must be fully prepared to fight the tyrants and the enemies of Allah as a prelude to establishing an Islamic state."** This bylaw is backed by Surat 9, verse 5, known as "the verse of the Sword." Chapter III: *"Terms of Membership"* in Article 4, (Section I) states the pledge and allegiance required by all international MB members: "I pledge allegiance to the Almighty Allah to constantly uphold and safeguard the principles of Islam, to fight in the cause of Allah, to adhere to the terms and duties of the brotherhood's membership, showing as much as possible obedience to Just leaders in sorrow and joy as long as it does not involve disobedience to Allah, I pay allegiance and may Allah be my witness." Chapter IV defines the Muslim Brotherhood's three administrative bodies and their function in carrying out the organization's objectives. It is Chapter V in the bylaws that lists the terms and the conditions required of a nation's membership in the International Muslim Brotherhood Organization (MBIO) and states that the Nation *"Must adopt all of the group's (MB) approach."* The MB bylaws also set conditions and terms for Brotherhood emigrants in Article 54 "Brotherhood emigrants should be subject to the movement's leaders in the state wherein they reside." It is the *bylaws of the Muslim Brotherhood* that set the standards, conditions and terms that each MB member, emigrant, leader, and supporter must pledge allegiance to and adhere to as long as they live. I was told that once you take the MB pledge of allegiance, accept the terms and conditions set forth in the bylaws, and are approved by the MB chairman and/or the *Brother's Controller—General,* you are a member for life **(18)**.

The MB "**Master Plan**" for establishing a universal Islamic ummah dictated under Shari'ah law in both the twentieth and the twenty-first century is found not only in their bylaws but also in their **second** detrimental blueprint document ascertained by Swiss authorities in the residence of Youssef Nada, a prominent international leader of the MB for over fifty years and the director of the Al-Taqwa Bank of Lugano, Switzerland. Nada was arrested for filtering money to Hamas and al-Qaeda terrorist organizations. The document dated the first of December, 1982, titled *"The Muslim Brotherhood Project"* and consisting of only fourteen pages contained proof of a complete strategic "global Vision of a worldwide strategy for Islamic policy" plan by the Brotherhood to enforce a long-term infiltration and sabotage of all Western societies (Europe and the United States) **(19).** There are a number of key areas specified in this document that will raise your eyebrows and should have raised numerous red flags to all government agencies involved in America's national security. The following are just a small sample of the key and instrumental factors found within the document entitled "The Prophet":

- *Avoiding open alliances with known terrorist organizations and individuals to maintain the appearance of "moderation";*

- *Infiltrating and taking over existing Muslim organizations to realign them toward the Muslim Brotherhood's collective goals;*

- *Using deception to mask the intended goals of Islamist actions, as long as it doesn't conflict with Shari'ah law;*

- *Establishing financial networks to fund the work of conversion of the West;*

- *Cultivating an Islamist intellectual community, including the establishment of think tanks and advocacy groups, and publishing "academic" studies to legitimize Islamist positions and to chronicle the history of Islamist movements.*

- *Building extensive social networks of schools, hospitals, and charitable organizations dedicated to Islamist ideals so that contact with the movement for Muslims in the West is constant;*

- *Involving ideologically committed Muslims in democratically elected institutions on all levels in the West, including government, NGOs, private organizations, and labor unions;*

- *Inflaming violence and keeping Muslims living in the West "in a Jihad frame of mind";*

- *Supporting Jihad movements across the Muslim world through preaching, propaganda, personnel, funding, and technical and operational support;*

- *Instigating a constant campaign to incite hatred by Muslims against Jews and rejecting any discussions of reconciliation or coexistence with them;*

- *Collecting sufficient funds to indefinitely perpetuate and support jihad around the world.* **(20)**

Each of these key listings found in this influential and well defined "The Muslim Brotherhood Project" plus the "Bylaws of the Muslim Brotherhood" should be paramount in the counterintelligence strategies of not only the US but all nations throughout the world.

The **third** influential "Master Plan" document of the MB was written by Mohamed Akrarn, aka Mohamed Adlouni, who was not only a member of the Board of Directors of the Muslim Brotherhood but also a senior Hamas leader in the United States. Arkran prepared the document titled *"An Explanatory Memorandum on the General Strategic Goal for the Group in North America"* for their Shura Council **(21)** and dated May 22, 1991. Mohamed Akrarn, in his presentation letter to the MB Shura Council, made the following plea in defense of his well-thought-out and planned strategy for infiltrating and sabotaging the infrastructure of North America: "We have embarked on a new stage of Islamic activism stages in this continent (North America)" **(22)**. Akrarn asked the MB council and members who attended the conference to keep "in mind that what is between your hands is not strange or a new submission without a root, but rather an attempt to interpret and explain some of what came in the long-term plan which we approved and adopted in our council and our conference in the year 1987" **(23)**. The document was discovered during an FBI raid in 2004 in

Annandale, Virginia, at the residence of Ismail Elbarasse, who was taken into custody after being detained after he and his wife were observed by two off-duty Baltimore County police officers videotaping the Chesapeake Bay Bridge support structure. Elbarasse, a father of six, is described by the U.S. Department of Justice as a "high-level Hamas operative" who had failed to honor a warrant as a material witness in Chicago, Illinois, in regard to the funding of various Middle East terrorist groups. It is this document that was used as evidence in the largest terrorist funding trial: the US v the Holy Land Foundation

This is not a new strategy developed just in the twenty-first century by the MB's radical Islamist movement but one that dates back to the 1980s. Remember that the international terrorist organizations *Hamas*, was formed in 1987 by the leader of the Muslim Brotherhood of Palestine, and *al-Qaeda* was founded in 1988 by cofounders Usama bin Laden and Abdullah Yousef Azzam, bin Laden's mentor and teacher and an important figurehead and professor in the international Muslim Brotherhood movement. The Memorandum consists of five major sections with the first two explaining where it was derived from and asking the members of the Shura Council, "How do you like to see the Islam Movement in North America in ten years?" **(24)** The key defining blueprints and influential factors in the memorandum can be found in Sections three and four, *"The Concept of the Settlement"* and the *"The Process of Settlement,"* in which Akrarn describes the major phase of the Muslim Brotherhood jihad in America, which he sums in this one quote: "In order for Islam and its Movement to become 'a part of the homeland' in which it lives, 'stable in its land' . . . the movement must plan and struggle to obtain 'the keys' and the tools for this process in carry out this grand mission as a **"Civilization**

Jihadist" responsibility lies on the shoulders of Muslims—on top of them—the Muslim Brotherhood in this country." For **"the Ikhwan (MB) must understand that their work in America is a kind of grand Jihad in eliminating and destroying the Western civilization from within and <u>'sabotaging'</u> its miserable house <u>by their hands</u> and the hands of the believers so that it is eliminated and God's religion is made victorious over all other religions"** (25). Akrarn continues by elaborating that in order for this *"Civilization Jihad Process"* to be effective and successful "it will take a gradual merger between private work and public work." In Section 4 he continues by stressing that, "And in order for the process of settlement to be completed, we must plan and work from now (document dated May 22, 1991) to equip and prepare ourselves, our brothers, our apparatuses, our sections, and our committees in order to turn into comprehensive organizations in a gradual and balanced way that is suitable with the need and the reality. What encourages us to do that— in addition to the aforementioned—is that we possess 'seeds' for each organization from the organization we call for." Akrarn in this quote is referring to an America only governed by Shari'ah law. Akrarn lists, in an attachment, **twenty-nine active** key MB organizations and gives the specific title: *"A list of our organizations and the organizations of our friends"* that are active participants and front organizations to be used in performing their **"grand Jihad in eliminating and destroying the Western civilization from within and <u>'sabotaging'</u> its miserable house <u>by their hands.</u>"** Akrarn's key listed organizations are as follows:

- **Islamic Society of North America (ISNA)**

- **Muslim Students Association (MSA)**

- The Muslim Communities Association (MCA)

- The Association of Muslim Social Scientists (AMSS)

- The Association of Muslim Scientists and Engineers (AMSE)

- Islamic Medical Association (IMA)

- Islamic Teaching Center (ITC)

- North American Islamic Trust (NAIT)

- Foundation for International Development (FID)

- Islamic Housing Cooperative (IHC)

- Islamic Centers Division (ICD)

- American Trust Publications (ATP)

- Audio-Visual Center (AVC)

- Islamic Book Service (IBS)

- Muslim Business Association (MBA)

- **Muslim Youth of North America (MYNA)**

- **ISNA FIQH Committee (IFC)**

- **ISNA Political Awareness Committee (IPAC)**

- **Islamic Education Department (IED)**

- **Muslim Arab Youth Association (MAYA)**

- Malaysian [sic] Islamic Study Group (MAYA)

- **Islamic Association for Palestine (IAP)**

- United Association for Studies and Research (UASR)

- **Islamic Occupied Land Fund (OLF)** became the **Holy Land Foundation (HLF)**

- **Mercy International Association (MIA)**

- **Islamic Circle of North America (ISC)**

- Baitul Mal Inc. (BMI)

- **International Institute for Islamic Thought (IIIT)**

- **Islamic Information Center (IIC)**

The above twenty-nine listed organizations by the Muslim Brotherhood are each part of the "seeds" and "tools" they have founded and planted in their plan for ***"eliminating and destroying the Western civilization from within and 'sabotaging' its miserable house by their hands"*** and were listed as *"front organizations"* to be used by the Muslim Brotherhood in the US Government Exhibit 003-0085/3:04-CR-240-G in the *United States v Holy Land Foundation* terrorist finance trial to establish a North America ruled by Shari'ah law only. It is important to understand that in order to become an effective organization under the umbrella of the Muslim Brotherhood it and its founders and leaders are required to take (1) a pledge of allegiance to the MB, (2) to take the oath or creed (motto) of the MB, and (3) to obey the MB bylaws.

Allah is our objective. The Prophet is our leader. The Qur'an is our law. Jihad is our way. Dying in the way of Allah is our highest aspiration. — **Motto of the Muslim Brotherhood**

The Holy Land Foundation (HLF) was the largest Islamic charity in the United States, headquartered in Richardson, Texas. It was originally listed and known as *The Islamic Occupied Land Fund (OLF)*, one of the twenty-nine key "seed" organizations to act as a front in the MB plans to "**sabotage America from within.**" Recall previously discussed in this chapter the *MB Bylaws* and the document titled *"MB Project"* in which their blueprint was "Collecting sufficient funds to indefinitely perpetuate and support jihad around the world" and **"Using deception to mask the intended goals of Islamist actions, as long as it doesn't conflict with Shari'ah law" (26).** In December 2001 the US government designated HLF a terrorist organization, seized all of its assets, and closed the organization. In 2008, a federal grand jury in Dallas, Texas convicted HLF under the *"material support statute,"* which congress passed in 1996 following the attack and bombing of the WTC in 1993 as part of the US Antiterrorism and Effective Death Penalty Act (Pub. L. No. 104-132), on ten counts of conspiracy to provide, and the provision of, material support to a designated foreign terrorist organization; eleven counts of conspiracy to provide, and the provision of, funds, goods and services to a Specially Designated Terrorist; and ten counts of conspiracy to commit, and the commission of, money laundering. They also convicted five of its leaders who were also known leaders of the American MB organization and who served as leaders on other key listed organizations such as the ISNA, ISA**, MSA, and CAIR (27).** On May 27, 2009, the Department of Justice Office of Public Affairs released the following statement in reference to the gravity of this trial and its convictions:

> Today's sentences mark the culmination of many years of painstaking investigative and prosecutorial work at the federal, state, and local levels. All those involved in this landmark case deserve our thanks," said David Kris, Assistant Attorney General for National Security. "These sentences should serve as a strong warning to anyone who knowingly provides financial support to terrorists under the guise of humanitarian relief (**28**).

In addition to the *Holy Land Foundation*, numerous of these listed organizations have been proven to be charity fronts for supporting operative movements and funneling money to Hamas, al-Qaeda and other radical terrorist movements under the MB umbrella. Examples of just how positive and influential these MB-based organizations have been in infiltrating and planting the "***seed to sabotage America from within***" are (1) the *Islamic Society of North America* (ISNA), one of the largest and most active MB organizations in North America; (2) the *Muslim Students Association* (MSA), the first MB organization founded in America and the second largest and most active organization in America and the most threatening; and (3) *The Islamic Centers Association* (ICD) very active and the leader in their "settlement Jihad Phase." All three of these MB front organizations are well-known and perfect examples of Ahkran's comment that "We have a 'seed' for a 'comprehensive *Dawah*' " (In Islam the word *Dawah* is the practice and/or policy by which a Muslim conveys their Islamic message to non-Muslims). The ISNA was incorporated in the state of Indiana in **July of 1981** and "***America*** *from within"* has become the most prominent, influential and active arm in the MB: **"*Civilization Jihad Settlement Process for eliminating and destroying the Western civilization from within and 'sabotaging' its miserable house <u>by their own hands!</u>"*** In the largest terror-financing trial held in America in 2008, known as the *United States v Holy Land Foundation for Relief and Development (HLF)*, "Federal prosecutors named ISNA an unindicted co-conspirator in the prosecution of five officials" and "listed it among 'individuals/entities who are and/ or were members of the US Muslim Brotherhood.' " In addition to being listed by the federal prosecutors as an individual entity of the US Muslim Brotherhood in the Holy Land trial it was also noted that the North American Islamic Trust (NAIT) was one of its subsidiaries and it was also named in the courts listing of coconspirators. Upon reviewing the various documents presented by the prosecutors I noted that several of the key leaders and board members of NAIT also served in equal status positions in the ISNA. The following quote describes how ISNA and NAIT worked together in funneling money to Hamas:

> A government memo, used in the trial, explains how NAIT was used to funnel money to Hamas: *"ISNA checks deposited into the ISNA/NAIT account for the HLF were often made payable to "the Palestinian Mujahadeen," the original name for the HAMAS military wing. Govt. Exh. 1-174. From that ISNA/NAIT account, the HLF sent hundreds of thousands of dollars to HAMAS leader Mousa Abu Marzook, Nadia Elashi (defendant Ghassan Elashi's cousin and Marzook's wife), Sheikh Ahmed Yassin's Islamic Center of Gaza, the Islamic University, and a number of other*

individuals associated with HAMAS. Govt. Exh. 20-55, 20-56 **(29).**

ISNA registered as a nonprofit 501(c) (3) organization and has been holding well-organized and well-attended conferences within America for many years and each conference has had a profound list of speakers who promote Jihad against America. Listed on their conference programs have been such prominent known terrorist leaders such as Mousa Abu Marzook , currently holds the title of Deputy Political Bureau Chief of Hamas operating out of Cairo, Egypt, and the Egyptian Muslim Brotherhood cleric Yusuf al-Qaradawi, plus members from various other known radical Islamist groups. As religious-sponsored conferences, these radical Islamist front organizations have been able to provide key speakers from numerous Muslim Brotherhood organizations, terrorist group leaders such as Hamas, and other radical Islamist supporters because they are legally protected by the First Amendment of the American Constitution. FBI can only attend these known recruiting and podium speeches promoting terrorism against America and its citizens because one of our most cherished freedoms is freedom of speech; assembly of religious organizations are protected and enshrined in the US. However, one must realize this same cherished freedom is used by the radical Islamist and other radical religious groups. Keynote speaker US citizen and Palestinian activist Linda Sarsour spoke at the fifty-fourth Islamic Society of North America (ISNA) conference held in Chicago, Illinois, during America's Fourth of July 2017 weekend. She began her speech by making a special recognition to her mentor, motivator, and encourager, Sirai Wahhaj, who also was in attendance at the conference. In case you may have forgotten, Imam Sirai Wahhaj (Imam of At-Taqwa) was listed as an unindicted coconspirator in the

1993 World Trade Center bombing **(30).** Sarsour stated during her twenty-two-minute speech: "I hope, that when we stand up to those who oppress our communities, that Allah accepts from us that as a form of jihad. We are struggling against tyrants and rulers not only abroad . . . but here in the United States of America, where you have fascists and white supremacists and Islamophobia reigning in the White House." Sarsour, at this July 2017 conference, shared the dais with Rasmea Odeh, who you may remember was convicted in 1969 to a life sentence in Israel for the killing of two Hebrew University students in a strategically organized and planned terrorist attack in a supermarket in Jerusalem, and for the attempted attack on the British Consulate. Odeh was released in a prisoner exchange in 1979 and immigrated to the United States by hiding both her relationship to the radical Islamist terrorist movement, her crime and her incarceration. How she was able to falsify her immigration entrance into the United States is mind-boggling, as the 1969 terrorist attack and her sentencing to life in prison plus her release ten years later in a prisoner exchange for an Israel soldier captured in Lebanon were all reported by the international media. The good news is Odeh was convicted in federal court in Detroit for falsely procuring US naturalization and for the concealing of her previous conviction and incarceration in November 2014 and was sentenced to eighteen months in US prison, her US citizenship was revoked, plus she is to be deported at the end of her prison term to Jordan. The bad news is she was released on bail pending her appeal and therefore she has not served any of her eighteen-month sentence as of July 10, 2017, she cannot be deported, and she is able to be a keynote speaker at radical Islamist events such as the ISNA conference held in July of 2017—plus she served as a delegate to the 2016 Democratic National Convention and was praised as being a Bernie Sanders surrogate **(31)**. The ISNA is able to hold its conferences because it hails as a religious organization although its prime purpose and programs are based on their "political cause," as noted in the "Sunnah's of the Prophet Muhammad," their b**ylaws,** their documents "An *Explanatory Memorandum on the General Strategic Goal for the Group in North America***,"** and their *"*The Muslim Brotherhood 'Project**,"** all political causes toward their ***"Civilization Jihad Settlement Process for eliminating and destroying the Western civilization from within and 'sabotaging' its miserable house by their own hands"* (32).** One needs to never forget that Islam is both a religious and a political movement as established by the Prophet Muhammad following his great Hijrah to Medina (See chapter II, "The Hijrah"). There is no separation between church and state in Islam as the Divine Laws of state are dictated by Allah.

The government of Canada on the 19th of July 2017, stripped *ISNA-Canada* and their associate the *Canadian Islamic Trust Foundation* of their charitable status in the country of Canada following the Canadian Revenue Agency (CRA) audit revealed they were financing a Pakistani Militant group. Remember in 2008 ISNA-America and their associate the *Holy Land Foundation* and numerous leaders of the Muslim Brotherhood organization were found guilty in a US Federal court of providing financial support to the Hamas terrorist organization. And yet there are numerous American citizens and government officials who still claim "the ISNA is not a threat to America and is a peaceful charity organization"!

The Muslim Student Association (MSA) has proven to be another very powerful and influential front organization founded by and under the umbrella of the Muslim Brotherhood. The MSA is the first front, or "seed" as Akrarn referred to it, to be formed in the US and it is from this one organization that many of the listed front organizations were founded. MSA was established as a student organization on the campus of the University of Illinois in 1962 and has become one of the most influential and even visible recruiting tools for the Muslim Brotherhood and the radical Islamist movement in America. Noted in the US v. Holy Land Foundation trial document Bate # ISE-SW 1823/U002005: **"In 1962, the Muslim Students Union was founded by a group of the first Ikhwans (MB) in North America and the meetings of the Ikhwan became conferences and Students Union Camps."** In the year 2017 the MSA has well-established chapters on nearly every college campus in America. It is not only a religious organization but it is also a political organization promoting and intimidating young Muslims and non-Muslims on their "Civilization Jihad Settlement Phase." MSA clearly defines in Chapter II, Article 3, sections B and C of the MB bylaws: **"(B) Teach the movement's younger members to flourish with these principles and demonstrate the true meaning of religiousness as individuals and families; They endeavor to sow the seed of the true meaning of fraternity, full integration, and genuine cooperation among them for international Islamic consensus, aiming to create a new generation to understand Islam correctly acting in accordance with its provisions,** (C) guidance, and admonition, which is a sound approach suitable for Muslims in the fields of education, legislation, judiciary, administration, military life, economy, health, and governance" **(33)**. The following are MB organizations that have been formed under the umbrella of the *Muslim Student Association*: (1) *The Association of Muslim Social Sciences* (AMSS); (2) *The Association of Muslim Scientists and Engineers* (AMSE); (3) *Islamic Medical Association* (IMA); (4) *Islamic Teaching Center* (ITC); (5) *Islamic Audio-Visual*

Center (AVC); (6) *Islamic Book Service* (IBS); (7) *Muslim Youth of North America* (MYNA);(8) *Islamic Education Department* (IED); (8) *Muslim Arab Youth Association* (MAYA); and (9) *United Association for Studies and Research* (UASR). The MSA campus conferences have become vocal centers for key MB Islamic speakers promoting Jihad against Jews and Americans in an "Israel Apartheid Week" on several US college campuses. Remember there is no separation in Islam between church and state—religion and politics—and that the MSA has become a powerful recruiting tool for the MB "Global Civilization Jihad." *"The Muslim Brotherhood 'Project' "* states that **"**Infiltrating and taking over existing Muslim organizations to realign them toward the Muslim Brotherhood's collective goals" and **"using deception to mask the intended goals of Islamist actions, as long as it doesn't conflict with Shari'ah law." (34)** An excellent example of the Muslim Brotherhood using its front "seed," the *Muslim Student Association*, in America as a recruiting "tool" to recruit young Muslims for their cause, even in America, would be the former president of Egypt and a devout member of the Muslim Brotherhood, Mohammed Morsi, who was a student studying for his doctorate on the campus of the University of Southern California in the 1980s—proving once again that it is a very small world we live in and that America's infrastructure is very vulnerable.

A third very influential example of how the MB has used their founded front organizations as "seeds" and "tools" to infiltrate and *"sabotage **America from within and by their own hands"*** would be *The Islamic Centers Association* (ICA). The establishment of a Muslim settlement within America was the major concept of four major MB blueprints: the *"Muslims Brotherhood Bylaws,"* the *"Muslim Brotherhood Project,"* the

"Explanatory Memorandum: the General Strategic Goal for the Group in North America," and the *"The Methodology of Dawah—The Forum Publication IV."* Each of these MB documents place emphasis on the purpose and task of the Mosque and the Islamic Centers in America as an *"axis of our Movement"* **(35)**. The Mosque and the Islamic Centers throughout America and the world, as in the seventh century under the leadership of Muhammad, are powerful recruiting "seeds" and "tools" as well as training centers for the Muslim Brotherhood rhetoric and the radical Islamic movement. Great emphasis was placed on the dimensions and process necessary in establishing the ICA settlements under Shari'ah law. ICA was listed as one of the leaders in the twenty-nine Islamic organizations noted in the US v the Holy Land Foundation Trial. "The center (and/ or Mosque) ought to turn into a 'beehive' which produces sweet honey." For "from the Mosque, he (Muhammad) drew the Islamic life and provided it the world the most magnificent and fabulous civilization humanity knew" **(36)** and the "base for our rise and our *'Dar-al-Arqam'*" (covenant) to educate us, prepare us and supply our battalions in addition to being the 'niche' of our prayers." Akrarn clearly defines that "the center we seek is the one which constitutes the 'axis' of our Movement, the 'perimeter' of the circle of our work, our 'balance center,' the 'base' for our rise and our *'Dar-al-Arqam'* to educate us, prepare us and supply our battalions in addition to being the 'niche' of our prayers" and "The center ought to turn into a 'beehive' which produces sweet honey" *(37)*. Akrarn not only proceeds to list the keys and tools that the ICA is to play in establishing a settlement under Shari'ah law but he also describes the dimensions and processes necessary in establishing this Islamic settlement. Akrarn continues by stating that "the 'center' role should be the same as the 'mosque's' role during the time of

Allah's Prophet (Muhammad), Allah's prayers and peace be upon him, when he marched to 'settle' the Dawah in its first generation in Medina. From the Mosque, he (Muhammad) drew the Islamic life and provided it the world the most magnificent and fabulous civilization humanity knew" **(38).** This one quote defines the purpose of the Mosque and the Islamic Center so that "we possess 'seeds' for each organization from the organization we call for"—the twenty-nine plus MB organizations listed in the memorandum and the Holy Land trial. The Mosque and Islamic Centers throughout America and the world, as in the seventh century under the leadership of Muhammad, are powerful recruiting "seeds" and "tools" as well as training centers for the Muslim Brotherhood rhetoric and the radical Islamic movement. As religious centers they are protected by our Constitution. In Chapter II, Article 2, Section F of the bylaws of the Muslim Brotherhood, "The need to work on establishing the Islamic State (settlement), which seeks to effectively implement the provisions of Islam and its teachings" **(39).** The Muslim Brotherhood *"Project"* states that its goal is "Infiltrating and taking over existing Muslim organizations to realign them toward the Muslim Brotherhood's collective goals" and "Using deception to mask the intended goals of Islamist actions, as long as it doesn't conflict with Shari'ah law" **(40).**

The Washington-based MB influential and very powerful front organization in America is *The Council on American Islamic Relations* (CAIR), the largest Muslim-rights group in America. Attorney General Ronald Weich stated that both prosecutor evidence and testimonies presented at the US v Holy Land trial revealed that the founders of CAIR were members of the International Muslim Brotherhood's terrorist network Hamas. As a result of this valuable information CAIR was listed as an Unindicted

Coconspirator along with ISNA, NAIT, MSA, IAP, UASR, and ICNA in the US vs. Holy Land Federal trial. How powerful and influential has CAIR become in America? Members of CAIR received top priority as active instructors used by the US State Department, FBI, US Armed Forces, intelligence communities, the Pentagon, and Homeland Security. Consequently these entries in the US government opposed and blackballed and or *blocked* any instructors and/or lecturers who did not present Islam as a peaceful religion, who used any reference to the term Jihad (war) and/or radical Islamist and anyone who quoted from the Qur'an, the Sunnah/Hadith and/or Shari'ah law to justify their material and information. I can personally attest to that unless you were endorsed by CAIR and/or the Muslim Brotherhood your chances of lecturing and training in the US government, the US educational system, and US Military at all levels of intelligence training were denied and/or revoked even if you had received outstanding evaluations from students and directors and/or commanders of said US government organizations. My personal experience was that the Muslim Brotherhood's network of front organizations controlled and manipulated all operational intelligence and counterintelligence training in the United States. Members of CAIR were very active and influential in manipulating information and policies in the US immigration department, the US Civil Rights department, and the US media. An excellent book written by Paul Sperry and David Gaubatz titled *Muslim Mafia: Inside the Secret Underworld That's Conspiring to Islamize America* reveals how manipulative CAIR is in our intelligence and counterintelligence operations and policies. Four US Representatives, led by Congresswoman Sue Myrick of North Carolina, in October of 2009 requested that the US Department of Justice investigate the allegations made in Sperry and Gaubatz's book and submit to congress all recorded and documented evidence and testimonies from the US v Holy Land trial. Final results revealed that CAIR had a definite and active relationship with terrorist organization Hamas. Although CAIR was not established when the 1991 *"An Explanatory Memorandum on the General Strategic Goal for the Group in North America"* was approved by the MB Shura Council it was listed in the US Federal trial US v Holy Land Foundation as coconspirators. Both the evidence and testimonies revealed their involvement in the Holy Land Foundation fraud. Clearly defined in the MB "Project" document "Infiltrating and taking over existing Muslim organizations to realign them toward the Muslim Brotherhood's collective goals" **(41)**. Because of the Holy Land Foundation trial, it is now public knowledge that the major Muslim organizations in the United States are actually controlled by the Muslim Brotherhood or a derivative organization, and yet the MB continues, in 2017, to dictate and control the intelligence trainers and training material and the selection of US Military Imams.

Space only allowed me to elaborate on four examples of very active and influential MB organizations that are well known and deeply entrenched within the infrastructure of America. However, each of these four "seeds" and "tools" serve as perfect examples to Ahkran's comment that, "We have a seed for a 'comprehensive *Dawa"* (In Islam the word *Dawa* is the practice and/or policy by which a Muslim conveys their Islamic message to non-Muslims). Their Dawa /master plan consisted of a significant set of documents revealing the complete blueprints of the Muslim Brotherhood's strategic plans for conquering the world and establishing one universal ummah under Shari'ah law. . **What** is mind boggling is how such an important and well-defined document, *"An Explanatory Memorandum on the General Strategic Goal for the Group in North America,"* found during an FBI raid in America and dated 1991, describing not only the twenty tools being used by the radical Islamist movement within North America but also clearly listing twenty-nine well-established front organizations that they are using to accomplish their *"New Islamic Settlement"* is being ignored and brushed under the table.

The **fourth** influential published blueprint of Muslim Brotherhood's *"master plan"* to establish a universal Islamic ummah and to make it "possible only by building Islamic Movements in the Western countries" is found in the book written by Shamim Siddiqi titled *The Methodology of Dawah— The Forum Publication IV."* This particular radical Islamist "how-to" blueprint was published in Brentwood, Maryland, US, by *International Graphics* in 1989 and confiscated during a raid by government security organizations in both Europe and the United States. Shamim made the following recognition: "I dedicate this book to those da'ees (those individuals who perform the Dawah) who are struggling and waiting to lay down their lives for establishing god's kingdom on earth" **(42)** and quoted the following revelation from the Holy Qur'an, Surat 33: 23: *"Of the believers are men who are true to that which they covenanted with ALLAH. Some of them have paid their vow by death (in battle), and some of them still are waiting; and they have not altered in the least"* **(43).** In his introduction, Shamim clearly defines his ideology and the obligation of all Muslims for a "Dawah" of the Western countries:

> *The time has come to expose and put an end to these dirty games. This will be possible only by building Islamic Movements in the Western countries in the homelands of those who have caused and are*

causing incalculable loss to the Muslim world and casting baseless aspersions against Islam day in and day out The only option left to the Muslims of West now is to start Islamic movement in their respective country of domicile, reach the people of the land and invite them to the fold of Allah (SWT). It is also their need. The effect of this life-saving move of the Muslim Ummah, living in the West, would be of paramount importance **(44).**

Chapter IV in Siddiqi's book *The Process of Islamic Movement in An American Perspective* defines and gives a well-defined blueprint in *Section 4, where* Siddiqi describes the outcome of a *"peaceful resistance"* (infiltration) and in *Section 5,"The Fifth and Sixth stage of the Dawah is 'The Migration' and 'final struggle'".* Siddiqi in reference to America made the following declaration:

The Muslims living in America, as such, have a very important role to play. If they are really interested in seeing the birth of an Islamic State anywhere in the Muslim world, they have no choice except to put all their energies, talents and resources in building and strengthening the Islamic Movement of America. This is the only way for them (while living in America) to see their lifelong desire fulfilled. If they do not act right now in this direction, one would have reason to believe that they are simply nurturing wishful thinking and have no real desire in their hearts to see Islam securing a dominant position somewhere in this world(**45**).

The MB believed that its purposes in the West would be "**better advanced by the 'use of nonviolent, stealthy techniques.**" The four intelligence-confiscated documents discussed in this chapter—(1) the "*Muslim Brotherhoods Bylaws*," (2) "*The Muslim of Brotherhood 'Project, "* (3) "*An Explanatory Memorandum on the General Strategic Goal for the Group in North America,*" and (4) "*The Methodology of Dawah—The Forum Publication IV "*—clearly reveal how strategically planned, influential and effective the MB technique has been and is in "***infiltrating and sabotaging America from 'within.' "*** Please note that three of the "master plans" were WRITTEN AND INFORCED IN THE 1980s! The Muslim Brotherhood has clearly sought to establish relations with, influence, and wherever possible penetrate government circles in the executive and legislative branches at the federal, state and local levels: the law-enforcement community, intelligence agencies, the military, penal institutions, the media; think tanks and policy groups, academic institutions, non-Muslim religious communities, and other crucial areas in the existence and function of the infrastructure of America. The Brothers engage in all of these activities and more for one reason and one reason only: to subvert the targeted communities in furtherance of the MB's primary objective—the triumph of Shari'ah law throughout the world. The twentieth and twenty-first century Muslim Brotherhood is the influential root of the **Revival of the Radical Islamist Movement**.

I apologize for the redundant areas within this chapter but I have continued to stress the obvious based on legitimate documents, books, trial evidence and testimonies and the sacred text of the Holy Qur'an, the Prophet Muhammad's Sunnah, and the Hadith and Shari'ah law, and yet many Americans refuse to accept the facts out of either fear or denial. In my lectures I compare this to a small child who sits in the middle of the floor surrounded by adults and when you place a blanket over his/her head they immediately assume they have disappeared and that you cannot see them. But remember their expression and excitement when one of the adults removes the blanket and responds with "Boo!" The child loves to play the game until it discovers that they are not actually hidden from view of the adults but rather it is the adults who are hidden from their view. Remember the old Arab Proverb: ***"The Enemy of my Enemy is my friend to help me get rid of one enemy but they are still my enemy."***

NOTES:

1. Explanatory Memorandum on the General Strategic Goal for the Group in North America," Government Exhibit 003-0085 3:04-CR-240-G. (Retrieved 11/21/2017)

2. Many individuals try and claim that Hamas is not part of the Muslim Brotherhood but the following quote taken from Hamas Charter clearly defines the MB as being the founder of Hamas: *"The Islamic Resistance Movement is one of the wings of Muslim Brotherhood in Palestine. Muslim Brotherhood Movement is a universal organization which constitutes the largest Islamic movement in modern times. It is characterized by its deep understanding, accurate comprehension and its complete embrace of all Islamic concept of all aspects of life, culture, creed, politics, economics, education, society, justice and judgement, the spreading of Islam, education, art, information, science of the occult and conversion to Islam."*

3. http://mideastweb.org/hamas.htm) (Retrieved 2/15/2017)

4. Bylaws of the International Muslim Brotherhood http://www.investigativeproject.org/documents/misc/673.pdf. (Retrieved 3/12/2017)

5. Imam Shaheed Hassan Al-Banna, The *Way of Jihad: Complete Text by Hassan Al-Banna founder of the Muslim Brotherhood, http://actmemphis.org/MB-The-Way-of Jihad-by-al-Banan.pdf.* (Retrieved 2/17/2017)

6. Ibid. Imam Shaheed Hassan Al-Banna,

7. Ibid. Imam Shaheed Hassan Al-Banna

8. Sayyid Qutb, *"Milestone Along the Road,"* *(Ma'alim fi al-Tariq) Chapter IX* – A Muslims Nationality and Belief.

9. Ibid. Sayyid Qutb, *Milestones.*

10. *"By-laws of Muslim Brotherhood"* http://www.ikhwanweb.com/article.php?id=22687&re-search.php and/or *"Bylaws of the International Muslim Brotherhood"* http://www.investigativeproject.org/documents/misc/673.pdf. (Retrieved 1/22/2017)

11. Ibid. Sayyid Qutb *"Milestone Along the Road"* pg. 10-11.

12. Ibid. Sayyid Qutb, *"Milestone Along the Road"* pg.132.

13. Ibid. Sayyid Qutb, *"Milestone Along the Road"* pg.21.

14. Ibid. Sayyid Qutb, *"Milestone Along the Road"* pg.132.

15. Sayyid Qutb, *"Milestone Along the Road"* pg. 69.

16. Ian Johnson 2010, *"A Mosque in Munich,"* Published by Houghton Mifflin Harcourt in Boston, New York, pg. 117.

17. Ibid. "By-Laws of Muslim Brotherhood"

18. Ibid. "By -laws of Muslim Brotherhood"

19. The Muslim Brotherhood "The Project" (PDF) investigative-project.org. and at Poole, Patrick, "The Muslim Brotherhood

'Project' " and "The Muslim Brotherhood 'Project'", *Front Page Magazine*, May 11, 2006. http://archive.frontpagemag.com/readarticle.aspx?artid=4476 and http://archive.front-pagThe emag.com/readarticle.aspx?artid=4475. (Retrieved 4/12/2017)

20. Ibid. The Muslim Brotherhood "The Project".

21. The Shura Council consists of about 100 Muslim Brotherhood leaders who are responsible for all of the organizations' strategies, planning, controlling and monitoring its terrorist network, front organizations and charities, and charting, monitoring and enforcing the organizations' by-laws, projects, and designated phases. In other words all and any important decisions and/or resolutions must be approved and implemented by the Shura Council.

22. "An Explanatory Memorandum on the General Strategic Goal for the Group in North America", Government Exhibit 003-0085 3:04-CR-240-G. www.investigativeproject.org/document/20-an-explanatory-memorandum (Retrieved 1/12/2017)

23. Ibid. "An Explanatory Memorandum on the General Strategic Goal for the Group in North America."

24. Ibid. "An Explanatory Memorandum on the General Strategic Goal for the Group in North America"

25. Ibid. "An Explanatory Memorandum on the General Strategic Goal for the Group in North America"

26. Ibid. The Muslim Brotherhood "Project").

27. United States v Holy Land Foundation trial. https://www.gpo.gov/fdsys/pkg/PLAW-104publ132/pdf/PLAW-104publ132.pdf and https://www.justice.gov/opa/pr/federal-judge-hands-downs-sentences-holy-land-foundation-case)Ibid. (Retrieved 4/12/2017)

28. *"Holy Land Foundation and Leaders Convicted on Providing Material Support to Hamas Terrorist Organization"*, https://www.justice.gov/opa/pr/federal-judge-hands-downs-sentences-holy-land-foundation-case. The case was investigated by the Joint Terrorism Task Force, involving agents from federal, state, and local agencies including: FBI, IRS - Criminal Investigation, U.S. Immigration and Customs Enforcement (ICE), Department of State, U.S. Secret Service, U.S. Army Criminal Investigation Division, the Texas Department of Public Safety, and the Dallas, Plano, Garland and Richardson, and Texas Police Departments. In addition, the Department of Justice Criminal Division's Asset Forfeiture and Money Laundering Section provided assistance.

29. USA v. Holy Land Foundation for Relief and Development, et al,.3:04-CR-240-G, Government's Memorandum in Opposition to Petitioners Islamic Society of North America and North American Islamic Trust's Motion for Equitable Relief, (N.D. Tex. July 10, 2008).

30. Siraj Wahhaj, "The Muslim Agenda in the New World Order," Islamic Association of Northern Texas, Dallas, Texas, November 15, 1991. ""*Where ever you came from, you came to America. And you came for one reason- for one reason only – to establish Allah's deen*" which means

[Obedience to Allah's authority]. https://www.investiga-tiveproject.org/mosques/409/masjid-at-taqwa) (Retrieved 4/12/2017)

31. Merriam-Webster Dictionary surrogate is to appoint as successor, deputy, or substitute - https://www.merriam-webster.com/dictionary/surrogate. (Retrieved 4/20/2017)

32. Ibid. "An Explanatory Memorandum on the General Strategic Goal for the Group in North America."

33. Ibid. "By-laws of the International Muslim Brotherhood" http://www.investigativeproject.org/documents/misc/673.pdf (Retrieved 4/17/2017

34. *Ibid.* The Muslim Brotherhood "Project"

35. Ibid. "Explanatory Memorandum the General Strategic Goal for the Group in North America."

36. Ibid. "Explanatory Memorandum the General Strategic Goal for the Group in North America"

37. Ibid. "Explanatory Memorandum the General Strategic Goal for the Group in North America"

38. Ibid. "Explanatory Memorandum the General Strategic Goal for the Group in North America"

39. Ibid. "By -laws of Muslim Brotherhood"

40. *Ibid.* The Muslim Brotherhood "Project"

41. Ibid. "Muslim Brotherhood 'Project'"

42. Siddiqi, Shamim A., 1989. "The Methodology of Dawah – The Forum Publication – IV", International Graphics, Brentwood, Md. http://www.dawahinamericas.com/book-spdf/MethodologyofDawah.pdf (Retrieved 4/12/2017)

43. Ibid. Shamim, Siddiqi, "The *Methodology of Dawah – The Forum Publication – IV*".

44. Ibid. The Methodology of *Dawah* – The Forum Publication – IV"

45. Ibid. The Methodology of *Dawah* – The Forum Publication – IV"

II
THE HIJRAH, THE SOUL OF ISLAM: THE ROOTS TO THE BOND OF BROTHERHOOD

Ibn Khaldun : "in the Muslim community, the holy war is a religious duty, because of the universalism of the Muslim mission and (the obligation to) convert everybody to Islam either by persuasion or by force." In Islam, says Ibn Khaldun, the person in charge of religious affairs is concerned with "power politics," because Islam is "under obligation to gain power over other nations." (1)

The **Hegira** known as the **Hijrah**; in the Islamic faith the word *Hijra* translates to migration and it is a significant factor and a powerful authority for it marks the true foundation of both the Islamic faith and the Muslim ummah (community) as known in the twenty-first century. Because of the persecutions and threats by the pagan tribesmen in the Arab city of Mecca, and following the deaths of his devoted wife Khadijah and his uncle, Muhammad and his converts attempted their third migrations for their safety. The first migration to the mountain city Taif was not successful as the tribes of Taif refused to protect him and his converts; the second one to Abyssinia in Habash, now known as Ethiopia, was successful and the emigrants were able to establish a Muslim ummah (community) under the protection of the Christian king. **(2)** However, it is his third and last migration from Mecca to the Jewish tribe's oasis known as Yathrib in the year 622 AD that changed the fate of Islam and is the motivation and role model that is dictating the present-day radical Islamist movement. During my twenty-seven years of in-depth studies and work within the universal Islamic ummah I have had the opportunity to hear several Muslims refer to migration as *ghurba,* which translates to stranger and/or one banished from your homeland and becoming a stranger in a foreign country. When I sought an explanation as to the difference between the two words I was told that **Hijrah** means one who migrates permanently and for Islam and *ghurba* means to migrate but only for a temporary residence in a foreign land for Islam. All three of Muhammad's Hijrah's, migrations, were initiated to find protection for himself and his small band of converts and to initiate and spread his new religious faith.

For the Islamic community, Muhammad's migration, the *Hijrah,* is as important and as significant as the migrations made by Adam, Abraham, Jacob, and Moses, recorded in the Torah, Bible, and the Qur'an. Muhammad and his convert's migration to Yhathib have left a legacy that has been instrumental in the twenty-first century radical Islamists global Jihad. Following are sixteen significant legacies from this historical event that have influenced the radical Islamist Global Jihad movement and caused the attacks and brutality that America and the world are experiencing in the twenty-first century.

The *Hijrah* marks the beginning of Islam as a dual movement within the Arab desert tribal society for it became both a religious and a political movement. It is in Yathrib that Muhammad became not only the new converts' religious leader and spokesman but he also became elevated to the position of supreme leader and spokesperson for Allah and a great military leader. The religious aspect of Islam requires all Muslims to believe in only one God and Muhammad as the last prophet, the five pillars of Islam, and the importance of the *'Akhirah'* (afterlife). Political Islam dictates all Muslims' moral, ethical, social, political and religious behavior in which they must live within the Muslim global ummah and their relationship to nonbelievers as revealed in the Holy Qur'an and the Sunnah/Hadith and enforced by Shari'ah law. Why is this so important in the twenty-first century? Very, because it is the political codes and rules established by Muhammad in Yathrib that dictate the radical Islamist global Jihad movement. Islam became a primary force and increased in its number of converts not while Muhammad was a spiritual leader in Mecca but when he became a political leader and a warrior after the Hijrah. Islam, in just ten years, under the political leadership of the Prophet, became a powerful force that conquered not only mass territory but many tribes. Muhammad's life as a religious, political and military leader during and after the Hijrah has had an enormous effect on the twenty-first century radical Islamists beliefs, attitudes, and actions.

(1) Prior to his emigration to Yathrib, the Hijrah, Muhammad was an individual who was interpreting the Divine revelations and trying to find converts. It was while in Yathrib that Allah gave the distinction to Muhammad of being not only His chosen prophet and messenger but Allah also relegated Muhammad in Surat 33:40 of the Holy Qur'an with *"the seal of the prophet."* **The absolute primacy to all Muslims is that Muhammad was the one man on earth who was chosen by Allah to reveal His revelations, who was given the seal of the prophet, and the one chosen by Allah to be his messenger to all mankind.** Muslims believe that Muhammad was sent by Allah to restore the primordial faith of Abraham—total submission to God—and therefore, the word of God, the Holy Qur'an, was revealed to Muhammad for all mankind. Islamic scholars and close friends of Muhammad started recording their memories of the prophet's sayings, the Sunnah, and his customary practices and deeds, the Hadith, during his life in Medina and following his death in 632 AD. From 610 AD to 632 AD it was Muhammad whom Allah chose to reveal his new faith, Islam, submission, and his revelations to. It is these revelations that scholars recorded, within fifty years of his death, in Arabic that is known as the Holy Qur'an. Because Allah revealed His revelations to Muhammad in Arabic and Arabic is the language which Muhammad spoke, the Qur'an is only legal and accepted as true and sacred if it is in Arabic. For over one thousand, three hundred years Muhammad has been relegated to a role model for all Muslim men.

(2)   Because of the significance that the Hijrah played in
the foundation of the new Islamic ummah (community), *Dar-al-Islam*, Muhammad changed the calendar
year in which all Muslims throughout the world would
live by. The year 622 AD, the year that Muhammad
and his converts emigrated to Yathrib (Medina), marks
year one (1 AH, after the Anno Hijrah) and consists
of only 354 days instead of the Georgian calendar of
365 days **(3).** This change proved to be a very significant strategy for Muhammad, for now the celebrated
Islamic feast days would not fall on the pagan feast
days. But the most significant strategy in relevance
to this change reveals Muhammad's cleverness By
changing the calendar in which the Muslim warriors
adhered to and honored they were now free to attack
the Arab caravans and invade the Arab villages, the
infidels or nonbelievers, without violating the recognized months of forbidden warfare. The pre-Islamic
Arab tribal rule recognized four months out of the
year in which any form of fighting and/or attacks on
merchant caravans were forbidden. This rule allowed
the pagan caravans to travel and trade their merchan-
dise without fear of attacks and/or death and it allowed them to meet and worship their many gods in
Mecca. In other words, Muhammad and his warriors
were now free to attack their enemies (*Dar-al-Harb—*
infidels) without violating the old tribal desert rule.
When I asked a senior Islamic scholar his response
was No, *absolutely not true!* However, Surat 9, verses
35 and 37, found within the Holy Qur'an, add validity to my perspective's logic: ***"The number of months
in the sight of Allah is twelve (in a year) so ordained***

by Him the day He created the heavens and the earth of them four are sacred. That is the right religion so wrong not yourselves therein and fight the pagans." My logical conclusion in no way is meant to dishonor the Prophet Muhammad but rather to accentuate his strategic abilities as a warrior and leader for Allah. I also noted that because of the lunar year calendar, the Islamic sacred month of Ramadan, the lunar month of fasting and performing *thawab* (good deeds rewarded by Allah), does not fall only during the hot summer months but rather rotates throughout the calendar seasons. The creation of the Islamic lunar calendar made the Hijrah, Muhammad's migration to Medina, the epoch of the era as it marks the formation of the first *Dar-al-Islam*.

(3)   It was during this time that Muhammad changed the direction of prayer for all Muslims' from Jerusalem, the city recognized by the Jews and Christians, to Mecca and the Ka'ba *(qiblah)* in Mecca in Saudi Arabia. Allah's revelation found in the Holy Qur'an Surat 2:144: ***"To see the turning of thy face, (for guidance) Muhammad, to the heavens, now shall we turn thee to a qiblah that shall please thee. Turn then thy face in the direction of the sacred mosque (al-Masjid al-Haram); wherever you [believers] are, turn your faces in that direction. The people of the book know well that is the truth from their Lord. Nor is Allah unmindful of what they do."*** And in Surat 2:149: ***"From whencesoever's thou startest forth, turn thy face in the direction of the sacred mosque (al-Masjid al-Haram); that is indeed the truth is not***

unmindful of what ye do." The *qiblah* signifies the fixed direction that all Muslims must face during their *salah* (prayers), which is the Ka'ba in Mecca, Saudi Arabia. Allah in Surat 2:124-127 informs Muhammad that the Ka'ba in Mecca is to be the center for all Arabian trade, a place of worship, and sacred territory; therefore, no form of fighting was to be allowed in the area. In Verse 127 Allah revealed that the Ka'ba was constructed by Abraham and his first-born son Isma'il (regarded as a *nabi*, prophet, and an ancestor to the Prophet Muhammad).. Even today, it is recognized by Muslims throughout the world as a sacred territory and has a special area recognized as Abraham's Station. Mosques, throughout the world, have a *mihrab*, a wall niche, which indicates the direction of the *qibla*, as do all Middle East nations' foreign embassies. Since 624 AD, Muslims throughout the world pray five times a day toward Mecca and the Ka'ba. By all Muslims facing only one direction when they pray signifies unity within the universal Islamic ummah (community) and a pure connection with Allah (God). Many individuals assume that the Ka'ba is an object that Muslims worship or that they worship its contents, the black rock, but it represents a focal point and the structure which Abraham, the Arab patriarch, built. The established prayer time for all Muslims connects the believers to Allah and the *Qiblah* connects all of the believers to one another.

(4)   Muhammad in 622 AD built the first Islamic mosque in Yathrib, which became the model for all future mosques. It was an open space large enough for the

entire group of new converts to meet together with large bamboo trees used for a lattice roof—a place of prostration to God, *"Masjid,"* toward Jerusalem. The mosque was a community public and political meeting place that provided food and care for its members, a place to meet and pray, a place where Muhammad and his male converts met to plan their strategic attacks against caravans and Jihad against nonbelievers, and a place to store their weapons. After the completion of the mosque, which took seven months to complete, Muhammad built his home beside it. The first mosque did not have a minaret, a raised platform or a pulpit, as simplicity was its main architecture design. The *Adhan,* the Muslim call to prayer, was not initiated by a revelation from Allah but rather during one of the new convert's public meetings held in their new community center, the mosque. In 629 AD Muhammad had to rebuild a mosque on its original site after severe damage caused by the wars between the Muslim warriors and the tribes of Mecca. The majority of the mosques built throughout the world have been built and supported by the Muslim Brotherhood international terrorist organization. The *Al-Masjid an-Nabawi* also known as the *Prophet's Mosque* now stands on the site of the mosques built by Muhammad. This new structure is recorded as being one hundred times larger than the original mosque of 622 AD and a Saudi Arabian paper reported that it now can accommodate more than five hundred worshipers. This new mosque, the *Prophet's Mosque,* houses the tomb of the Prophet Muhammad (*pbuh*) under the Green Dome and is the second most sacred mosque in the world for all Muslims. The importance of the first Islamic mosque and the twenty-first century radical Islamist is that Muhammad as their role model used the mosque as his headquarters for war and a place to store weapons, for it was not only a place of worship for Muslims, as it is both a religious and political-movement community center. Even after Muhammad's death his successors continued to use the mosque as a storehouse for their weapons and the headquarters for their war strategies. The present day mosque is both a community worship center, meeting place, educational facility, and government and justice (Shari'ah law) facility, preaching Jihad (war), and the storing of weapons. In other words, the Islamic world was ruled and controlled from the mosque.

(5)   Muhammad's elevation to supreme judge and leader of the new Islamic community also marks the beginning of a legal structure out of the ethical and moral principles found within the Qur'an and Muhammad's Sunnah (words), recorded within the Hadith. Even from the age of a young boy Muhammad was called *Al-Amin,* the trustworthy, and was respected for his integrity. He was approached by the Jewish tribal leaders of Yathrib, who sought his help as mediator to help them solve their tribal confrontations and in return they promised him and his persecuted converts safety and refuge. In Yathrib, Medina, Muhammad's mission was to establish a moral reform of legislation within the nomadic tribal traditions and to become the arbitrator and the source of all authority.

An authority that no longer was to be administered through their tribal leaders but was to be transferred to Muhammad from Allah (God) as '*His chosen messenger*'. Like Moses after the Jewish exodus, Allah gave Muhammad the laws of ethics that were required within the behavior and well-being of this new Islamic community. These laws of ethics that determine what is right and what is wrong by Allah's will are referred to as the **"Divine Law" or** Shari'ah law, "*A way.*" For each Muslim, their submission to Allah's Divine Laws is a personal conscious act for their own individual welfare in this life and their next life. It was by Muhammad, acting as executor, legislator, and judge for the Islamic ummah that instructed and enforced the laws of Allah " ***Shall I seek for judge other than Allah? When He it is who hath sent unto you. The book, explained in detail . . . The Word of thy Lord doth find its fulfillment in truth and in justices: None can change His words for He is the one Who Heareth and knoweth all"*** (6:114 & 115). In the Islamic legal system there is only one source of pure authority and that source is Allah; therefore, Islamic law, Allah's laws, cancel out all man-made legal systems. It is from the legacy of Muhammad and the second most sacred text the Sunnah recorded in the Hadith, that the Islamic legal codes and rules for the lives and moral behavior for all Muslims is found. Also found in Muhammad's legacy are the restrictions and rules of war being revised by the twenty-first century radical Islamist. I was not able to find, in my years of research, any written codes of law to be recorded at this time accept what was recorded in the Sacred Hadith. What I did discover during this research and living and working within the Islamic universal ummah is that **the Islamic state did not create the laws but rather the laws created the state of Islam**. Allah is the head of the state of Islam and the source of all its laws and Muhammad, as Allah's messenger, on Allah's behalf, translated and enforced those laws. It is the extreme "Divine Law" Shari'ah law, that was revealed to Muhammad only after the Hijrah emigration that dictates the extreme behavior of the radical Islamist and they are using that to justify their acts of brutality and violence.

(6)   The Hijrah not only marks the turning point in Muhammad's life from the role as a religious leader to that of a political leader and a great warrior but also it marks a turning point in the revelations that he received from Allah. It is this turning point that dictates and controls the mind-set and ideology of the present day Jihadist. The Quranic poetic verses which speak of mercy, compassion, kindness, and *"no compulsion in religion,"* found in Surat 2:246 and 2:256-257 were revealed to Muhammad while he was a preacher striving to gain new converts in Mecca and prior to his emigration to Yathrib, before the Hijrah. It is during Muhammad's life in Yathrib, renamed later in Islamic history "the city Medina" or Madinat Rasul Allah, means "City of the Prophet of Allah," that Muhammad received the Jihad revelations dividing the world between good, *Dar-al-Islam*, and evil *Dar-al-Harb*. This also marks the point in Islamic history not only when Muhammad's role is

changed by Allah, but also when all previous revelations found in the Qur'an became abrogated, replaced, by the new revelations of war and conquest.

(7) In Islamic history, Muhammad's Hijrah is recognized as equal to **Moses's Hijrah**, for both prophets were commanded by God to lead their people from persecution and bondage in an Arab country to a place where God had destined them to be. I often heard the Muhammad's Hijrah referred to as *"The Muslim Exodus*!" Both Moses and Muhammad made their historical emigrations by and under the direct command of God and both prophets provided their refuges direction and safety under the leadership of God and as God's chosen messengers. The Hijrah of the early Muslims has the same historical and religious significance as the twenty-first century Hijrah in the Western world, including America—Muslims who are being forced to emigrate from persecution and bondage. However, unlike Muhammad's Hijrah, the twenty-first century Muslims are emigrating from persecution and bondage being forced on them by individuals of their own Islamic faith—their brothers in Islam. Allah, in Surat 49:10, said: *"The Believers are but a single Brotherhood. So make peace and reconciliation between your two brothers, and fear Allah, that ye may receive mercy."* Ustadh Abdullah Yusuf Ali's scholarly translation of this verse reads: "The enforcement of the **Muslim Brotherhood** is the greatest social ideal of Islam. On it was based the Prophets Sermon at his last pilgrimage, and Islam cannot be completely realized until this ideal is achieved*"* **(4)**.

The big question that no one seems to want to ask and/ or answer is why? Why would their **brothers in Islam** be persecuting and forcing them to emigrate? And why has the universal Muslim ummah not condoned this action, which is against the revelations of Allah, and why have they not provided them, their brothers in Islam, with safety and refuge? Is this new twenty-first century Hijrah, under the leadership and enforcement of the radical Islamist, a desecration of a historical and sacred religious event for all Muslims throughout the world? Muhammad declared, in the Hadith, that migrating to a non-Muslim country was considered to be one of the seven major sins unless one migrates to a non-Muslim land to promote Islam and to bring new converts to Islam. The individual quality of migrating for personal reasons is promised *hellfire*; however, the individual who migrates to promote Islam and gain converts is promised the ultimate reward of the perfect afterlife. The important factor that so many individuals seem to miss or deny is that **migration, for the radical Islamist, is part of the doctrine of their global jihad.** Usama bin Laden compared his forced expulsion from his home land of Saudi Arabia, first to Sudan and then to Afghanistan, to the Prophet's forced *exodus* from Mecca to Medina known in Islam as *"**The Muslim Exodus**"*—the *Hijrah*. An elderly Pakistani gentleman told me "that his forced emigration from India to Pakistan, because he was being persecuted as a Muslim, was his Hijrah, the same as the Prophet Muhammad's "By comparing their event to that of the Prophet's journey and referring to it as *"**The Muslim Exodus**,"* bin Laden was able to resonate in the minds of young Muslims throughout the world to join al-Qaeda and fight in the Prophet's declared Global Jihad. Muhammad's migration, Hijra, from Mecca to Medina is the migration that leads to the creation of Jihad, *as a war*, a revolution against nonbelievers. One must also remember that it was the introduction of Jihad *as a war* that made Muhammad and his new Islamic ummah, community, triumphant as warriors for Allah. Prior to Muhammad's Hijrah, he convinced individuals in Mecca to join his new faith by kindness and preaching; however, after the Hijrah to Medina Muhammad became a warrior and spread his new faith by the sword. It is this second phase in Muhammad's life that has promoted and enforced the ideology for the twenty-first century radical Islamist psychological warfare. Part of their ideology and strategy is to inflict mass migration to designated *Dar-al-Harb* lands, lands of war (nonbelievers), such as Europe, America, Canada, and Africa to immerse themselves into the local politics, education, economy, and social structures (infiltration). The Islamic Jihad doctrines of a divided world between *Dar-al-Islam* (land of Islam) and *Dar-al-Harb* (land of war) or good versus evil was established through the revelations of Allah during the prophet's life in Medina, also known as the *Hijra period*. The second key factor in the twenty-first century Hijrah (migration) can be traced to Allah's revelations revealed to Muhammad that He and He alone had created the earth and the heavens: ***"He created the heavens and the earth in true (proportions). He makes the night overlap the day, and the*** *day overlap the night; He that subjected the sun and the moon (To His law)"* (39:5). The Prophet, peace be upon him, said: "The earth has been made for me (and for my followers) a place for praying and a thing to perform Tayammum, therefore anyone of my followers can pray wherever the time of a prayer is due" **(5).** Islam is both a religion and political movement and therefore their political aim is to bring the Shari'ah law to all *Dar-al-Harb* lands. *"**Allah created all of the earth for Muslims".***

(8)   Muhammad united the Arabs in the region and formed the first Islamic ummah (community) which was based on the tribal traditions of the period. The establishment of this new social/religious community was very important if Muhammad was to establish order and Islam as a united faith in a community that was predominantly Jewish. The ummah established a dual purpose for it established a political order for the new converts who had left their families, clan, and tribe to follow Muhammad and it established a religious community under the governing authority of God.

(9)   For Muhammad declared a **brotherhood** between the new immigrants and the local Muslim who were living in Yathrib in order to integrate them. Muhammad called the immigrants 'mhuaji '(plural *muhajirun*) because of their belief that they were descended from Abraham through Hagar as well as the importance which he ascribe to the Hijrah. The *Muslims* who were living in Medina prior to the Hijrah were

called *Ansar,* or helpers. I recall being told that even the Bedouin who joined Muhammad as warriors and members of his raids were called muhajirun for they were also emigrants to Yathrib. The original historical name for brotherhood was *mu'kh't'*. In the Holy Qur'an, reference is made to their earlier situation when it says, **"Remember when you were enemies. God has united your hearts and through his grace you have become brothers"** (3:103). Bin Laden used Muhammad's strategy in forming a brotherhood with various tribes, for example the Taliban and Pashtun tribes in Afghanistan. In a drafted letter to Nasir al-Wuhayshi, Bin Laden wrote, "We must gain the support of the tribes who enjoy strength and influence before building our Muslim state!" **(6)** Muhammad, as a religious and political statesman, became successful because he formed a brotherhood or total solidarity, *asibiyya*, with other Arab tribes. The most powerful aspect about Muhammad's forming of this Muslim brotherhood is that it was formed by conviction and not by brutality and/or force as it promised its member's prosperity and survival in this world and salvation in the next. A lesson obviously not learned and/or accepted by the radical Islamist, who considers them to all be members of a brotherhood because of their brutality and ability to dehumanize all non-believers. **"The emigrant, Yathib, the Prophet went there as an emigrant. And that there was a strong bond between him and the indigenous believers, despite the absence of any blood relationship"** (33:6). Muhammad believed that the individual's rights and obligations were always defined by their subordination to the ummah (community) interest. A belief that is still held to be a doctrine of truth in the twenty-first century Islamic universal community.

(10)   Young Muslim fighters from around the world have joined the radical Islamist movement as mujahidin because they believe they are called by Allah to fight in the **Great Battles** that will mark the end of times, **apocalyptic, and restore** *the Soul of Islam*. Muhammad prophesied this *Great Battle* would take place in the remote village of Dabiq in northern Syria: "The Last Hour would not come until the Romans (who were Christians) would land at al-A'maq or in Dabiq (in Syria). An army consisting of the best (soldiers) of the people of the earth at that time will come from Medina (to counteract them)" **(7).** The radical Islamist believes that Muhammad's prophesy is now coming true and that the **Great Battle** between the invading Christians and the defending Muslims, in which the Muslims are the victors, is now being played out.

> The Prophet said: It will turn out that you will be armed troops; one is Syria, one in the Yemen and one in Iraq. Ibn Hawalah said: Choose for me, Messenger of Allah, if I reach that time. He replied: Go to Syria, for it is Allah's chosen land, to which his best servants will be gathered, but if you are unwilling, go to your Yemen, and draw water from your tanks, for Allah has on my account taken special charge of Syria and its people **(8).**

The self-proclaimed caliphate Abu Bakr al-Baghdadi, echoing bin Laden's rhetoric, has used Allah's revelations to Muhammad, as recorded in the Hadith, that the *Great Battle* between the Christians and Muslims will occur in al-Sham as a successful recruiting tool. Muhammad commanded his warriors in Medina that they were to conquer the territory of **Bilad al-Sham;** in Arabic it means "land of the North." In the seventh century there were no borders separating territories and establishing individual nations; the territory was mass and open to all Bedouin. Abu Bakr al-Baghdadi declared once he became Caliph that there would be no borders in Muhammad's claimed **Bilad al-Sham.** If you recall the border between Iraq and Syria was destroyed and in 2017 ISIS is threatening the borders of Jordan and the Golden Heights of Israel. The territory known as al-Sham consisted of the modern-day regions of Iraq, Syria, Lebanon, Israel, Jordan, Palestine, Cyprus, and the Turkish Hatay Province. This territory is also referred to as *the Levant,* which is why ISIS also referrers to itself as ISIL, the Islamic State of the Levant. Al-Sham is the territory that Allah revealed to Muhammad: **"Behold, indeed the heart of the abode of the believers is al-Sham" (Ahmad), and "The heart of the abode of Islam is al-Sham"** (Tabarani). I do not believe that Americans have fully comprehended exactly what Usama bin Laden, Abu Bakr al-Baghdadi, and the twenty-first century radical Islamist mean when they claim they are taking back their Levant territory. They are following Allah's command as revealed to Muhammad that the land was theirs from the great conquering Jihads by their forefathers. All of this territory claimed as al-sham (Iraq, Syria, Lebanon, Israel, Jordan, Palestine, Cyprus, and the Turkish Hatay Province) must be restored under the Islamic state prior to the end times, the *Great Battles* (apocalyptic). Muslims believe that the antichrist will appear in the empty region between Syria and Iraq, which marks the same territory that al-Qaeda and ISIS have needed to claim. All of this territory was owned and under Islamic rule (Shari'ah law) in the Muslim conquest during the middle of the seventh century (634) and called the Islamic Province of Bilad al-Sham. I recall being told by several Muslims with great pride that, "the Islamic empire extended two hundred days journey from east to west, from India to the shores of the Atlantic Ocean." Abu Bakr al-Baghdadi stated that Islam is only taking back the Bilad al-Sham which is rightfully theirs. All of this territory was also under the Ottoman Empire, which was an Islamic Empire and all of its Sultans were Caliphs under Islamic law until 1922. According to Islamic Law, once a territory is under Islamic rule (Shari'ah law) it always is an Islamic territory. The radical Islamists are following Allah's and Muhammad's commands given during the Medina period or the Hijrah period (as several radical Islamist have referred to it), and secondly reclaiming what is rightly theirs by the Divine laws of Allah. The reconquering of the Al-Sham territory by the radical Islamist universal movement (1) will reinstate Allah's revelation and Muhammad's prophesy of the *Great Battle* and victory for the universal Islamic victory; (2) return the soul of Islam; (3) be an effective recruiting tool; (4) execute of the divine command and duty of all Muslims to establish a world ruled by the Divine Law—Shari'ah law; (5) all mujahidin who have sacrificed their lives for Allah's cause will receive an afterlife of eternal bliss; and (6) **this great victory will prove to the universal Islamic ummah and the world that Allah has truly chosen the Muslims as His chosen people.**

(11) The land of the Levant/al-Sham has a second significant factor for the radical Islamist, for it is this territory in which Allah proclaimed and Muhammad prophesied that the *Great Battles* (apocalyptic) will precede the **Day of Judgment, the end of time.** Radical Islamists have used the Muslims' fear of the *Day of Judgment* as a motivational tool to entice youth from around the world to join Allah's cause before it is too late. Why is this so important to a Muslim? Muslims believe that their life on earth is merely a test as to how and where they will live their afterlife. On the *Day of Judgment* only Allah will determine where each individual will spend his or her afterlife, either in eternal fire or in eternal bliss. Allah in Surat 99:6-8 informs his believers that they must not be afraid of death, for in the end they will return to Allah who created them; however, in this same passage Allah warns that each individual will be held accountable for their deeds on earth (good versus evil). It is from this revelation that bin Laden, when asked about the killing of innocent people on the brutal attack of the World Trade Center, 9/11, responded that it was not for him to decide who was good and who was evil,

that only God could make that decision. Belief in the end-times and the *Day of Judgment* is mandatory of all believers in Islam and is listed as the fifth article of faith. It is this fear factor that the radical Islamists have used to create a cult of **shahid,** martyrdom, **"*for if ye are slain, or die, in the way of Allah. Forgiveness and mercy from Allah are far better than all they could amass "*** (3:157-158). Muhammad, peace be upon him, said the following in reference to martyrdom:

> The person who participates in (Holy battles) in Allah's cause and nothing compels him to do so except belief in Allah and His Apostles, will be recompensed by Allah either with a reward, or booty (if he survives) or will be admitted to Paradise (if he is killed in the battle as a martyr). Had I not found it difficult for my followers, then I would not remain behind any sariya going for Jihad and I would have loved to be martyred in Allah's cause and then made alive, and then martyred and then made alive, and then again martyred in His cause.. **(9)**

For the Muslim youth the promotion of a death cult mentality in which the elevated status of *shahid* (martyr) is exalted by both Allah and Muhammad is the ultimate goal of each Jihadist. Much thought and premonition is experienced in reference to their afterlife, as Muslims believe "**To God we belong and to God we shall return!**" *(Qur'an, Surat 2:156)* The above quoted verse is also recited when a Muslim dies. In this revelation Allah clearly states that as the creator all mankind belongs to Him and Him alone. Believers in Surat 29:3 of the Holy Qur'an are warned that just reciting they believe in Allah, the Shahada, *"There is no God but Allah, and Muhammad is his messenger"* is not enough. *"Do men think that they will be left alone on saying 'We believe' and that they will not be tested?"* ISIS has quoted this revelation many times to justify their killing of Muslims. The Shahada is the first of the Five Pillars of Islam. Besides Allah's revelations concerning death and hellfire and the last *Day of Judgment* one can also find many prophesies relating to the subject from Muhammad as recorded in the sacred text of the Sunnah/Hadith during His Medina period, or *Hijrah period,* as many Muslims refer to this Islamic historical period. Muhammad, peace be upon him, kept replying to the emigrants (believers) who were digging a trench around Medina to protect it from the Mecca tribes (nonbelievers). **"O Allah, there is no good except the good of the Hereafter; so confer Your Blessings on the Ansar and the Emigrants" (10).** There are three primary apocalyptic ideologies that play a major role in the minds and hearts of Muslims throughout the world: (1) they have the opportunity to be part of the last Great Battle to restore the soul of Islam; (2) to restore the Islamic ummah as established by Muhammad in Medina, and (3) to have the guarantee from Allah and Muhammad of an afterlife of bliss and paradise. Each of these three ideologies are important calling cards for Muslims throughout the world.

(12) One of the largest branches within Islam and considered to be the most orthodox is called Sunni or "trodden path" or "the way," because they are the followers of the path of the Prophet Muhammad. The proper name of the Sunni is *Ahl al-Sunnah wa'l-Ijma or* **people of the Sunnah.** The name is derived from the Sunnah, "is the sense of divinely inspired words of Muhammad," and "is the second source of Shari'ah law" **(11).** Sunni adhere to the divinely inspired behavior and words of Muhammad found within his Sunnah/Hadith. The reason for this is that although Islamic Law is recognized as deriving from both the Qur'an and the Sunnah in actuality, upon studying Islamic Law I learned that it is the legacy of Muhammad that dictates, for the Sunni, their moral, social, religious, Jihad (war) and political legal issues. The prophet declared in his farewell sermon: "O People, no prophet or apostle will come after me, and no new faith will be born. Reason well, therefore, O people, and understand words which I convey to you. I leave behind me two things, the Qur'an and my example, the Sunnah, and if you follow these you will never go astray" **(12).** The Sunni have four religious jurisprudence, legal, schools. The Sunni was the largest branch of Islam that formed at Muhammad's death and established the first Caliphs to succeed Muhammad—Abu Bakr. Unlike the Shiites, the Sunni accept the legitimacy of the first four Caliphs who preceded Muhammad. They believe that at all other Islamic religious sects, such as the Druze, the Twelve

Imams, and the Shiites, are not devote Muslims as they have departed from many of the original beliefs as found within the Qur'an and the Prophet Muhammad and refer to them as being innovators of the truth. Why is this important in understanding the twenty-first century radical Islamist Global Jihad? **One**, the following radical Islamist terrorist organizations are Sunni: the Muslim Brotherhood, al-Qaeda, ISIS and their global terrorist network. **Two,** it is the Sunni terrorists who have been targeting the Shiite communities, mosques, and leaders because in their beliefs they are not true Muslims and also they are trying to re-instate the old war between the two sects that dates back to 632 AD. **Three,** it is the Sunni who are dedicated to restoring 'the soul of Islam', the Islam as founded by Muhammad in the seventh century. **Four**, the Sunni adhere to and follow Islam as taught by Wahhabi, the eighteenth century reform of sociomoral reconstruction of Islam. **Five**, the Sunni are the largest and strongest Islamist branch in the world. **Six,** the first appointed successor to Muhammad in 632 AD was the Sunni Caliph Abu Bakr, which also happens to be the name that the new twenty-first century ISIS self-proclaimed Sunni Caliph Abu Bakr al-Baghdadi chose to be known as. **Seven**, the Sunni radical Islamist movement believes they are following the divine inspirations and prophesies of the Prophet Muhammad and the end of times—the Day of Judgment. **Eight, the Sunni believe that Muhammad bridges the gap for all mankind between God and the temporal world.**

(13) Jihad, prior to Muhammad's Hijrah in 622 AD, was defined only as the *spiritual struggle within oneself against sin,* also known as the Greater Jihad. The second type of Jihad, *a struggle or fight against the enemies of Islam*—the Lesser Jihad—was not in existence until after the Prophet Muhammad's emigration to Medina. The traditional tribal raids of the Arab peninsula were replaced by Allah's call for Jihad (a *struggle or fight against the enemies of Islam).* The radical Islamist mujahidin argue that they are merely modeling their lives as warriors of Allah. They believe that the first Islamic ummah, founded by Muhammad in Medina in 622 AD, followed strict Divine religious rules and were a strong guerilla military force ever ready and eager for battle—Jihad. By emulating the actions and mind-set of the early Muslims and their role model Muhammad, the twenty-first century mujahidin believe they are enforcing justice as obligated by Allah's revelations. Their belief is based on the actions and sayings of the Prophet Muhammad and his commitment to the new Islamic community: "My livelihood is under the shade of my spear, and he who disobeys my orders will be humiliated" **(13).** Allah's revelations, recorded in the Holy Qur'an, and Muhammad's deeds and thoughts, recorded in the Sunnah/Hadith, portray Jihad as a *struggle or fight against the enemies* and characterize Islam as the divine instrument that is to make all individuals in the world believers. In the Holy Qur'an, Surat's 47, 48, and 49, are known as the *Three Medina Surat's* and deal with the organization of the Muslim ummah (community) in regard to both external and internal

relations and are known as the *Hijrah Books*. In Surat 47, titled *"Muhammad,"* Allah directs the Prophet on the necessity of preparing for battle and fighting against his foes. It was during the first year of the Hijrah that Muhammad and his converts were under threat of extinction. It is from Surat 47 and Surat 49 that the present day Jihadist and their leaders quote most of their rhetoric. For example, Allah in verse 4 in Surat 47 directs Muhammad and his converts that once their fight (Jihad) has begun that they are to fight with vigor and brutality. *"Therefore, when ye meet the unbelievers smite at their necks; at length, when you have thoroughly subdued them bind (the captives) firmly."* But Allah also makes it very clear that *"He could certainly have exacted retribution from them; but (He lets you fight) in order to test you, some with others. But those who are slain in the way of Allah, He will never let their deeds be lost."* It is in the beginning of their battle against the nonbelievers that there will be "a great loss of life but after the enemies' numbers are thinned down, prisoners may be taken" (**14**). Allah, in Surat 47, verses 1-19, assures Muhammad and his converts that He will guide them and is with them and that they are to show aggression and hostility toward their enemies in the name of Allah and their faith. The aggression and hostility that the radical Islamist jihadist is inflicting on their victims (enemies) is a reenactment of the seventh century warriors under the leadership of the Prophet Muhammad. The second group of revelations during the period of the Hijrah, and recorded in Surat 48, are believed to have been revealed to Muhammad about 628 AD and inform the Muslims that their victory will come from their devotion to their faith, courage, patience, and perseverance. "Allah grants His Mercy on a far higher standard than man in his limited horizon can see." The third group of the three Medina Surat's is titled **"Al-Hujurat"** and is believed to have been revealed to Muhammad in 9AH. Allah stresses the importance that the new Muslim ummah must show respect to Allah's chosen prophet, **"Allah's Messenger."** For example, the Quranic poetic verses which speak of mercy, compassion, kindness, and **"no compulsion in religion,"** found in Surat 2:246 and 2:256 & 257 were revealed to Muhammad while he was a preacher striving to gain new converts in Mecca and prior to his emigration to Yathrib, before the Hijrah. After the Hijrah, the Quranic revelations in Surat 3:85 and in Surat 9:5 revealed **"there is only one religion and that is Islam"** and gave all Muslims the right to **"kill all nonbelievers wherever they find them." "If anyone desires a religion other than Islam (submission to God), never will it be accepted of him; and in the Hereafter he will be in the ranks of those who have lost (All spiritual good)"** (Surat 3:85). In Surat 9:5 it states there is only one religion and that is Islam and to kill all nonbelievers, also known as *the verse of the sword*. As set forth by Muhammad and accepted in Islamic law the world is divided into good (*Dar-al-Islam*) or evil (*Dar-al-Harb-war*). In other words, the radical Islamists and their proclaimed Global Jihad are merely fulfilling and supporting the right and correcting the wrong as set forth in the seventh century by Allah and enforced and proclaimed by Muhammad. In Surat 47:4 Muhammad was known as intercessor for humanity; but the present day Islamist dwells only on his leadership and his life as a great warrior and conquer. The great fourteenth century Arab scholar Ibn Khaldun stated: "Only he who has gained superiority over a nation or a race is able to handle its affairs. The religious law would hardly ever make a requirement in contradiction in the requirements of existence"**(15)**. Until Muhammad's proclamation - "A section of my community will continue to fight for the right and overcome their opponents till the last of them fights with the Antichrist!" **(16)** is reached **it** is the obligation of the universal Muslim ummah (community) to fight (Jihad) against the world of evil or the *Dar-al-Harb*, the world of war. Radical Islamists believe that the **world is their battlefield!** Why? Because it was migration that led to the creation of Jihad in Medina. And **it was Jihad that made Islam triumphant.**

(14) The radical Islamist (al-Qaeda, ISIS, etc.) have incorporated a *Black Flag* as an emblem of their symbolic bravery and their historical connection to the Hijrah and to Prophet Muhammad's emigration. Thawban said that The Messenger of Allah (sawas) said: "The black banners come from the east, as if their hearts are like pieces of iron, so whoever hears about them then go to them so give allegiance to them, even if crawling on ice because indeed amongst them is the Caliph, Al Mahdi!" **(17)** Several of Muhammad's companions made reference to "the black banners coming from the east" before the coming of the Mahdi, Messiah,

and the end of times. The historical legends and scholarly reports of the Prophet's life as a religious/political leader and warrior describe the black banners and his warriors being clad in black. The flag displayed by the radical Islamist is totally black with the *Shahada,* declaration of faith, written in Arabic in white across the top: ***"There is no god but Allah [God]. Mohammad is the messenger of Allah."*** Underneath the *Shahada* is a white circle, representing the seal of the Prophet, inscribed in black Arabic ***"Mohammed is the messenger of God."*** The black banner or flag calls attention to the life of the Prophet Muhammad as a great warrior and his conquering of an empire in the name of Islam. Historical legends and scholarly reports of the Prophet's life as a religious/political leader and warrior describe his warriors being clad in black and "carrying the black flags from the east." This is very significant as Abu Bakr Baghdadi, ISIS's new self-proclaimed Islamic Caliph, is a descendent of the Prophet Muhammad and has chosen the black flag with the seal of the Prophet, as did the early Caliphs following Muhammad's death. The black banners/flags have become effective recruiting tools and powerful propaganda symbolizing the radical Islamist as true warriors of Allah who are inspired by and who are following the war tactics and strategies as set forth by their forefathers in the seventh century and that they are blessed with the seal of the Prophet Muhammad. This one factor alone establishes the fact that the radical Islamists have declared their war against America and the world to be strictly a religious war not political war. **Good versus Evil!**

(15) The Hijrah is to depart from one territory to another because of persecution or to emigrate for Allah and to spread Islam. Muhammad, the first Hijrah, traveled from the city of Mecca, where he and his religious converts were persecuted, the land of war or *Dar-al-Harb*, to the city of Medina, also a land of war (*Dar-al-Harb*), but where individuals were receptive to him and his new religious converts and provided them with housing, aid, and protection. During this journey Allah spoke the following message to Muhammad: "***Was not the earth of God spacious enough for you to flee for refuge?***" (4:97) Allah promised not only Muhammad but all Muslims that, "**Those who migrate for the sake of God shall find many places for refuge in the land in great abundance**" (Qur'an Surat 4:99-100). I learned during my work and friendships with Muslims from various nations that they believed, "Allah had promised them that every part of this earth was created by Him and therefore every corner of earth **is** one universal Islamic ummah (community) and that Allah never formed borders to separate nations or to prevent them from entering." Muhammad and his new converts' emigration has become a role model for the present day mass Muslim refugee emigrants from Syria and Iraq. Like the Prophet, they too are fleeing from persecution and oppression and are seeking asylum in territories that have been declared by many of their religious and political leaders as the land of Jihad (war). Allah and Muhammad both proclaimed it to be the duty of every Muslim, **by peace or by force, to transform the infidels of *Dar-al-Harb* into a *Dar-al-Islam*, a land**

ruled only by Shari'ah law. During my work, travels, and studies I heard an elderly Imam, in 1995, state that like Allah had commanded the Jews while they were in exile so he commanded the Muslims in exile to build houses, take advantage of the wealth and prosperity within that nation, marry infidels, and have many sons and daughters and increase in numbers for in doing this you will increase the number of Muslims in that nation and provide more opportunities for Muslims to enter that nation and establish a larger and stronger Islamic ummah. In the book of Jeremiah, found in the Holy Bible, Chapter 9:4-9, God commanded the exiled Jews in Babylon under the rule of Nebuchadnezzar, a descendent of Isma'il, Abraham's son by the Egyptian maid servant Hagar, to:

> *Build houses, and settle down, plant gardens and eat what they produce. Marry and have sons and daughters; find wives for your sons and daughters in marriage, so that they too may have sons and daughters. Increase in number there; do not decrease* (18).

I found this most interesting as this is the concept of the *Civilization by Jihad* that the Radical Islamists promote and is part of the Muslim Brotherhood document *"An Explanatory Memorandum on the General Strategic Goal for the Group in North America,"* "Phased Plan," dated May 22, 1991. Migration, *Civilization by Jihad*, is a major part of the Muslim

Brotherhood strategy phase listed in their *Expanding the Muslim Presence in America* document which states by *"birth rate, immigration, and refusal to assimilate"* **(19)**. See chapter I, "Muslim Brotherhood" and chapter V, "Psychological Warfare." There is no difference between the warriors of the seventh century and the warriors of the twenty-first century, as both have emigrated from territories considered to be *Dar-al-Harb*—infidels/nonbelievers. Islamic law, Shari'ah law, binds all individual Muslims to one universal Islamic community, not to a specific territory. Islamic law states that any territory can be acquired by either force or by peace and can only receive the title of *Dar-al-Islam*, land of Islam, if all of its inhabitants are ruled only by Shari'ah law. In lieu of today's mass migrations of Muslim refugees it is very important to understand the collation between the historical migration of Muhammad and the migration **Civilization Jihad** of the twenty-first century. Unfortunately, this *phase plan* has proven to have been very effective in Europe and in North America. I mentioned this several times during my lectures, briefings, and meetings with American academia and government officials and was laughed at. In fact, I mentioned this during my lecture at Queen Ann's College at Oxford University in Oxford England in 2007 and received very rude and insulting comments from fellow American scholars. I had the honor and opportunity to meet and speak with an elderly Pakistani Muslim who proudly explained to me how his trip, and that of his fellow Muslim exiles' journeys, from India to Pakistan, Indian Independence Act 1947, was their

"Hijrah, just like the Prophet Muhammad, Peace be Upon him, in 632 AD. " As a role model it is important to note that by the end of his first year in Medina Muhammad had built the first Islamic mosque, created an Islamic calendar, made Islam not only a religious movement but also a political movement, and established a strong military force with a large supply of weapons. What is interesting to note is that it was the same Jewish and Christian tribes, infidels/nonbelievers, that had offered Muhammad and his converts aid and protection and who had sought him to be a peacemaker within their oasis that he set war against and thus established a powerful and ruling Islamic community. Muhammad's ultimate goal was to destroy and take over Mecca, the city, and the citizens who had rejected and persecuted him and who had forced him to emigrate. **Muhammad, 622 to 632 AD, had established the first Islamic community *Dar-al-Islam* and the first *Dar-al-Hijrah* on earth by both aggressive action and by enforcing Allah's revelations.** This historical event marks in Islamic history the first emigration by the first Muslim refugees and therefore it has become not only the model and motivation but also a major strategy and priority being effectively used by the twenty-first century global Jihad movement. Majid Khadduri, in his book *War and Peace in the Law of Islam,* wrote a chapter on Islamic Law and Muslims who immigrate into a non-Muslim territory:

> If the Muslim entered *Dar-al-Harb*, land of war or land of infidels, without 'aman', (diplomatic immunity) he is under no

obligation to observe its laws and regulations as those under 'aman. In Muslim
legal theory, the Muslim in a non-Muslim
territory without aman is at war with that
territory. He is, therefore, under no obligation to submit to the law of non-Muslim territories . . . If the Muslim, however, enters
Dar-al-Harb by permission of the imam,
he may seize property or take prisoners of
war in the same way as the Jihadist" **(20).**

The power found in this quote and Islamic law is
"If the Muslim entered Dar-al-Harb, land of war or
land of infidels, without 'aman (diplomatic immunity
grant of security), he is under no obligation to observe its laws and regulations as those under 'aman."
Muhammad, peace be upon him, stated: "Indeed
actions are but by intention, and each will be rewarded according to his intent. So whose goal is to
migrate for Allah and His Messenger, his migration
is for Allah and His Messenger, and whose aim is to
migrate to some worldly gain or to take the hand of
a woman in marriage, his migration is to that which
he has sought" **(21)**. It was by migration that the religion of Islam became not only a religious movement
but it was transformed into a powerful religious and
political force not only in the Arab region but also
throughout the world. In order to fulfill the radical
Islamist goal and vision of restoring the **soul of Islam**
and to reenact Muhammad's historical journey they
have initiated a **Civilization Jihad** that incorporates
mass immigration, infiltration, and fear by savagery

and propaganda. I personally refer to the twenty-first century Global Jihad mujahidin as *"revolutionary missionaries."*

(16) The **Cult like** behavior and strong bond of brotherhood among the warriors of the seventh century under the leadership of Muhammad is duplicated today among the twenty-first century radical Islamist warriors. There are many distinctive duplicated cult behaviors found between these two different centuries warriors of Allah: (1) they both display an excessively zealous, even fanatical, commitment to Allah's revelations and to Muhammad's teachings from the period of the Hijrah; (2) the display of being the elitist even to an exalted status; (3) the extreme willingness to die for Allah—martyrdom ((*shahada*); (4) they have a polarized us-versus-them mentality (*al-amr bi'l-maruf* good versus evil); (5) they justify their brutality and savagery based on the revelations of Allah and Muhammad's words and deeds good versus evil; *"There has to be a nation among you summoning to the good, bidding what is right, and forbidding what is wrong, it is they who are the felicitous"* (3:104); (6) they have devout loyalty to their leader, Muhammad—whether dead or alive, remembering that the Caliph represents Muhammad and Islamic law; (7) they have devout loyalty to the brotherhood—warriors of Allah (the cult); (8) they have devotion to the mission of procuring the universal Islamic ummah (community); (9) they have an obligation to the global spread of Islam as commanded by Allah and Muhammad—a revolutionary missionary mind-set;

and (10) they have a willingness, even an eagerness, to commit acts of violence not acceptable to a civilized society. Can the above ten similarities of the mind-set and behavior of the seventh century Islamic warriors and that of the twenty-first century Islamic warriors be disputed?

The Arabic word Hijrah, translates to migration it is not only a key historical factor for all Muslims but it is also the significant foundation and motivator for Muslims around the world. Because of its significance in establishing who is the radical Islamist it is very important to have an understanding of their interpretation of the *Hijrah* and how much it has and is influencing and controlling their declared universal war, a Global Jihad, against the land of war or *Dar-al-Harb* or land of nonbelievers. (1) It was Muhammad's migration, the Hijrah, from persecution in Mecca to the Jewish Oasis of Yathrib, now known as Medina, in 622 AD that marks the true beginning of the Islamic era and its calendar. The living legacy for the radical Islamist is built on the life of Muhammad as both the religious and political warrior for the new converts. (2) Year one for the universal Muslim ummah, community, is marked by the year of Muhammad's Hijrah—622 AD is 1 AH (year of the Hijrah). For the radical Islamist it marks the year in which Allah established Muhammad and Islam as the supreme religious movement that is to conquer and rule the world. **(3)** Muhammad established a set daily prayer schedule, five times a day, for all Muslims that connects the believers to Allah in unison; (4) It was not until the Hijrah that the absolute primacy of Muhammad was established as the only man on earth who received *"the seal of the prophet"* and who was declared as the last prophet (messenger) from Allah. The living legacy for the radical Islamist is built on the life of Muhammad as the last messenger prophet, the religious leader, the legislator, the political leader, and the great warrior and strategist for Allah's newly established Muslim ummah (community). (5) For it is this sovereignty that has forced the radical Islamist to be constantly at battle with Western media and authors who in their opinion have insulted the prophet and his supremacy as Allah's chosen messenger. Freedom of speech is not an accepted attribute found within the radical Islamist movement or in Shari'ah law. An excellent example of the importance of Muhammad in the universal Islamic ummah is the attacks in Paris and Niger in response to the Charlie Hebdo's published depictions of Muhammad. These publications were not an insult to the Islamic ummah, community, but rather they were an insult to Muhammad, the last and greatest of the chosen prophets of Allah. I quickly learned, in the beginning of my twenty-seven years of experience in the universal Islamic ummah, that **Muhammad bridges the gap for all Muslims and all mankind between God and the temporal world**. (6) Muhammad under the guidance of Allah established the first Islamic ummah (community). This new ummah mentality established a dual purpose for it established a political order for the new converts who had left their families, clans, and tribes to follow Muhammad, and it established a religious community under the governing authority of God. It is this strong survival mentality based on the mind-set that good-versus-evil or them-versus-us (non-Muslims-versus-Muslims) ideology that is motivating the twenty-first century radical Islamist. This strong brotherhood concept, of the seventh century, and the us-versus-them ideology is taught in the Islamic *madrassas*, Islamic schools, throughout the world. (7) What is the radical Islamist interpretation of just what Allah's will was for this newly established seventh century Islamic community? And why is this important? Because it is the historical interpretation of the seventh century and Muhammad's first Islamic community that dictates and controls their goal and vision for not only the twenty-first century universal Islamic community but also for the world. (8) For the radical Islamist fighting for *the "soul of Islam"* is fighting for the return of the Muslim ummah as established by Muhammad in the seventh century. The Muslim ummah dictated the moral and ethical codes by which all individuals must live by according to the Divine Laws of Allah and that *"there is no God but Allah and that Muhammad is his last messenger."* (9) Because of the migration and Muhammad's responsibility as the newly emigrated converts leader and protector he developed a dual life—that of their religious leader and as their political leader. It was Muhammad's political role as a great military strategist and warrior that has influenced the present-day radical Islamist and has become the ideology that dictates the radical Islamists' vision of Allah's will for the world. They believe that Muhammad would be honored and that he would praise them for their acts of savagery and brutality. It is the following Sunnah that the radical Islamists have based their ideology on: Muhammad, peace be upon him, stated, "My livelihood is under the shade of my spear, and he who disobeys my orders will be humiliated" *(22).* In other words they are striving for Muhammad's approval as he plays a major role in their life here on earth and their life in the hereafter. He is their hero and role model! (10) Because Muhammad represents the gap for all mankind between Allah and temporal man he became the executive, legislative, and judicial leader and spokesman for the universal body of Islam. It is therefore important to understand that Allah is the head of the state of Islam and is its source of all governing authority. Because the Divine Law, the law dictated by Allah and interpreted by

Muhammad for all mankind is supreme and just over any laws created and executed by temporal man it is the governing factor for the radical Islamist—the perfect law. In Islam it is the Divine Law, Shari'ah law, which dictates and regulates the life and thoughts of all mankind. (11) "The Caliphate in reality is a substitute for Muhammad in as much as it serves, like him, to protect the religion and to exercise leadership of the world" **(23).** As the substitute for the prophet Muhammad, he is the administrator and the enforcer of the Divine Law—Shari'ah law—and therefore he is the chief advisor of all Islamic civil and military decisions. In the minds and hearts of many Muslims Abu Bakr al-Baghdadi, the self-proclaimed caliph of ISIS, is a substitute for Muhammad and Baghdadis call for Muslims throughout the world to fight against the infidels is a direct order from Allah and Muhammad. Abu Bakr al-Baghdadi bridges the gap for all mankind between God and the temporal world. (12) Prior to the Hijrah, the Islamic converts prayed toward Jerusalem, the religious center for the Jewish, Christian, and Muslim followers and the city of Allah (God), Torah, and the Bible. But it was during Muhammad's life in Medina that he turned against the Jews and the Christians, and he received the revelation from Allah directing him and his followers to pray toward the Ka'ba located in Mecca, located in Saudi Arabia. This is very significant to the Islamic faith as the Ka'ba is historically recorded as being built by the patriarchs Abraham and his son Isam'il. (13) Muhammad declared that all Muslim converts declare their allegiance and total submission of faith to Allah, known as the **Al-Shahada**: "There is no god but Allah and Muhammad is the prophet of Allah." (14) It is by and because of the Hijrah and the **us-versus-them** ideology that Allah commanded Muhammad to establish a (revolutionary) religious movement in which **the world is divided into two sectors: Da-al-Islam (land of Islam)** and *Dar-al-Harb* (land of war/land of non-believers). This revolutionary religious movement, the second Jihad or the Lesser Jihad, is a war against all non-Muslims—a Global Jihad in which the world is to be ruled only by Allah's Divine Law— Shari'ah law. (15) The twenty-first century radical Islamist mujahidin (warriors) strong bond of brotherhood, a **Cult like** behavior, is a replica of the bond among the warriors of the seventh century under the leadership of Muhammad. (16) Both the Holy Qur'an and Muhammad's Sunnah, found within the Hadith, stress that as believers of Islam they are **obligated to fight in Allah's declared war** against the world of non-Muslims. For the radical Islamist it is this new Jihad, Jihad by war, which dictates and motivates the radical Islamist movement to spread Islam and conquer the world by fighting (9:5). (17) What is the radical Islamist interpretation of just what Allah's will was for this newly established seventh century Islamic community? And why is this important? Because it is the historical interpretation of the seventh century and Muhammad's first Islamic community that dictates and controls their goal and vision for not only the twenty-first century universal Islamic community but also for the world. (18) As found within the Holy Qur'an and the sayings of Muhammad and the example set by the seventh century Islamic revolutionary, Jihad is the overruling concept that no compromise is permitted in their declared *"just war"* against all nonbelievers, for one either converts to Islam, agrees to be ruled under the Shari'ah law (Divine Law), or dies. (19) For the radical Islamist the Hijrah is interpreted to depart from one territory to another or to emigrate for Allah and to spread Islam. I learned during my work and friendships with Muslims from various nations that they believed "Allah had promised them that every part of this earth was created by Him and therefore every corner of earth **is** one universal Islamic ummah (community) and that

Allah never formed borders to separate nations or to prevent them from entering." Allah's revelation is found in the Holy Qur'an Surat 4:97: *"Was not the earth of God spacious enough for you to flee for refuge?"* Both the warriors who emigrated to join Muhammad in Medina and those who have emigrated to join the twenty-first century radical Islamists stress no compromise in restoring *the soul of Islam* and the belief that they are sanctioned by Divine Order. (20) Muhammad established the recognition that Muslim warriors who died in battle fighting for Islam would receive paradise as martyrs. Last but not least, (21) prior to the Hijrah, Allah's revelations to Muhammad were of peace and *compassion*, *"no compulsion of religion";* however, following this historical emigration, Allah's revelations spoke of war and He divided the world between good and evil. But the important factor that dictates the difference between Allah's revelations between the Mecca period and the Medina period of Muhammad's life is the distinction that the later revelations (Medina period) abrogate, replace, the previous revelations (Mecca period).

It is paramount that the world accepts and comprehends the importance and power which the Hijrah plays in the mind-set, ideology, and the psychological warfare strategies that the radical Islamist have declared in their global Jihad (war) against all nonbelievers. **The Hijrah migration of today is an imitation of Muhammad and his refugees in 622 AD for migration is part of the doctrine of Jihad. Revising Islam to its original status as established by Muhammad after the Hijrah is the responsibility of all Muslims.** Both the warriors who emigrated to join Muhammad in Medina and those who have emigrated to join the twenty-first century radical Islamists stress no compromise in restoring *the soul of Islam* and the belief that they are sanctioned by Divine Order. The prophet Muhammad, peace be upon him, made the following statement: "The (whole) earth has been made a mosque (or a place of prayer) and a means of purification for me, so wherever a man of my ummah may be when the time for prayer comes, let him pray" **(24).** The Hijrah has a comprehensive meaning that is understood in Islam and by all Muslims.

NOTES

1. Ilbn Khaldun, *The Muqaddimah: An Introduction to History.* trans, Rosenthal, Princeton University Press, 1967, *P. 183.*

2. In Psalm 68:31 "Ethiopia shall soon stretch out her hands unto God" and Homer in *Iliad* speaks of the "blameless Ethiopia".

3. The Hegira took place in AH 1. So, the year 2017 on the Christian Calendar is AH 1438 on the Hijriah Calendar.

4. Taken from the scholarly notes of the late Ustadh Abdullah Yusuf Ali of the Holy Quran. Ustadh Abdullah Yusuf Ali is the only scholarly translation and notes that have been approved and accepted by the Royal decree # 19888 dated 16/8/ 1400 AH issued by the Custodian of the two Holy Mosque King Fahd ibn Abdul Aziz. The Holy Qur'an, reverence 4928, pg.1591.

5. Sahih al-Bukhari *Hadith Book 7, #335,* narrated Jabir bin `Abdullah.

6. Draft Letter of Usama bin Laden to Nasir al-Wuhayshi, Harmony Program, Combating Terrorism Center at West Point, https://www.ctc.usma.edu/. (Retrieved 4/12/2017)

7. Sahih Muslim. Book 54. The Book of Tribulations and Portents of the Last Hour. Chapter 9) The Conquest Of Constantinople, The Emergence Of The Dajjal And The Descent Of 'Eisa bin Mariam. Hadith 44.

8. Abu Daud, Hadith, Book 15, Number 7, Narrated, Imran ibn Husayn: https://sunnah.com/abudawud/15. (Retrieved 4/16/2017)

9. Ibid. Sahih al-Bukhari, Hadith, Vol. 1, Book 2, #35, Narrated by Abu Huraira,

10. Ibid. Sahih al-Bukhari, Hadith, Book 56, #51, Narrated Anas:

11. Coulson, N.J. M.A., 1964, 'A History of Islamic Law', University of Edinburgh Press, Pg. 56.

12. The Prophet Muhammad's Last Sermon, this sermon was delivered on the ninth day of Dul Hijjah 10AH in the Uranah valley of Mount Arafat (in Mecca) http://www.islamicity.com/mosque/lastserm.HTM. (Retrieved 4/12/2017)

13. Sahih Bukhari, Volume.4, Chapter 88, "The Book of Jihad," (Fighting for Allah's Cause), Narrated Ibn Umar, https://issuu.com/shahidmahmud/docs/sahih-al-bukhari-volume-4-ahadith-2/109. (Retrieved 4/16/2017)

14. Ibid. Taken from the scholarly notes of the late Ustadh Abdullah Yusuf Ali of the Holy Quran. Rev. 4821, Pg. 1560.

15. Ibid. Ibn Khaldun, Pg. 160.

16. Abu Daud, Hadith, Book 15, Number 8, Narrated Imran ibn Husayn: https://sunnah.com/abudawud/15. (Retrieved 4/16/2017)

17. "The authenticity of 'the black flags' coming from the East", retrieved 11/09/2017, http://www.islamweb.net/emainpage/index.php?page=showfatwa&Option=Fatwald&Id=101399 (Retrieved 6/12/2017)

18. The Holy Bible, Book of Jeremiah, Chapter 29, verses 4 & 5.

19. Muslim Brotherhood, An Explanatory Memorandum on the General Strategic Goal for the Group in North America, "Phased Plan," dated May 22, 1991, a document entered into evidence in the US v Holy Land Foundation, *Shariah The Threat to America – An Exercise in Competitive Analysis p Report Team BII,* The Security for Security Policy, Washington, D.C., pg. 273 and http://www.investigativeproject.org/document/20-an-ecentury explanatory-memorandum- -on-the-general.pdf. (Retrieved 6/22/2017)

20. Khadduri, 1955, *War and Peace in the Law of Islam,* Chapter XVI, *"Muslims in Non-Muslim Territory"*, The John Hopkins Press, Baltimore, Maryland.

21. Sahih al-Bukhari, "The Book o Bad'al-Wahy", Vol.1/9, Hadith 1, and "Sahih Muslim", "The Book of al-Imaara", Vol.3/1515, Hadith 1907.

22. Ibid, Sahih Bukhari, Volume.4, Chapter 88, Narrated Ibn Umar.

23. Ibid. Ibn Khaldun, pg. 155.

24. Ibid. Sahih Bukhari, 335.

III
AN IDEOLOGY BASED ON RELIGION
PURIFICATION AND FIGHTING FOR THE SOUL OF ISLAM/DYING FOR ALLAH

"The only religion in the sight of Allah is Islam."
(Holy Qur'an, Surrat 3:19)

Philosopher Destutt de Tracy referred to ideology as a "science of the mind." As used within this chapter, an *ideology* is a set of beliefs and ideas that not only influences but motivates the ways in which a particular group, in this case the present radical Islamic network, behaves and thinks, and even their unconscious habits of mind. The radical Islamist ideology is based on their literal and seemingly narrow interpretation and concept of the sacred texts of Islam: the revelations of Allah as recorded in the Holy Qur'an, the sayings and deeds of the Prophet

Muhammad as recorded in the volumes of the Sunnah, and the Hadith and the Shari'ah law (the Divine Law of Allah). What is so very important for the reader to understand is that they, the radical Islamists, believe they have a monopoly on the correct and only understanding and interpretation of the legality of each of these important sacred Islamic texts. For Islam, as I learned during my many discussions with the Imams, is not just a religion but it is a complete way of one's daily life, a life in which the believer must submit their whole being to the *"Oneness of Allah,"* the *"Oneness of mankind,"* the *"Oneness of the Message,"* and the *"Oneness of Allah's messenger,"* the Prophet Muhammad, Peace be upon him. In Islam there is no separation between church and state for it was during the seventh century and following Muhammad's night journey known as the *Hijrah* that Islam became both a religion and a political movement. It is this total and unquestionable belief that is the motivation and controlling factor of WHO, HOW, and WHY Muslims have become radicalized.

> *__In order that ye (O men) may believe in Allah__ __and His Messenger, this ye must assist and honor__ __him and celebrate His praises morning and night.__ __Indeed, those who plight (pledge allegiance or__ __oath to you, [O Muhammad] – their fealty (ac-__ __tually) pledging their allegiance to Allah..__ The hand of Allah is over their hands. Then say one who violates his oath, does so to the harm of his own soul, and one who fulfills what he has Covenanted with Allah will soon grant him a great reward* (48:9 & 10).

An explanation is required here to help you, the reader, understand why I have placed such an emphasis on these two revelations and the present day radical Islamist mujahidin. The Muslim warriors in the seventh century came with such great enthusiasm and respect for the prophet Muhammad that their allegiance to him was undeniable. This same enthusiasm and undeniable allegiance is found today in the universal twenty-first century radical Islamist mujahidin. The word Caliph in Arabic is *Khalifa,* which means successor—the religious and political successor to Muhammad and therefore, like Muhammad, becomes the leader of the universal Islamic ummah. To the mujahidin who have pledged their allegiance to Abu Bakr al-Baghdadi, the self-proclaimed Caliph of ISIS, they have pledged their allegiance to the Prophet Muhammad. Allah in the above quoted revelations gave strict instructions to all Muslim converts that they were to *"**assist and honor him and celebrate His praises morning and night**"* and they were also directed that they must *"**pledge their allegiance or oath to you (O Muhammad).**"* But Allah also made it very clear in this same revelation that by pledging their allegiance or oath to Muhammad or his successor(s) they were *"**fealty (actually) pledging their allegiance to Allah.**"* This is a powerful insight as to WHY young Muslims from throughout the world are so willing to have this opportunity to prove their allegiance to Allah, to Muhammad, and/or his successor (the *Khalifa*). The following quote taken from the Hadith adds credence to the importance of the pledge of allegiance for Islam and to the Prophet: "We entered upon Ubada bin As-Samit while he was sick. We said, 'May Allah make you healthy. Will you tell us a Hadith you heard from the Prophet and by which Allah may make you benefit?' He said, 'The Prophet called us and we gave him the pledge of allegiance for Islam, and among the conditions on which he spoke the Pledge from us, was that we were to listen and obey (the orders) both at the time when we were active and at the time when we were tired, and at our difficult time and at our ease and to be obedient to the ruler and give him his right even if he not give us our right, and not to fight against him unless we noticed him having open Kufr (disbelief) for which would have a proof with us from Allah" **(1).**

Additional significance in the previous quote from Surat 48, verse 10, is the importance of "**The hand of Allah is over their hands.**" A tradition founded in the Arab tribal culture is the placing of one's hands over that of the tribal leader's hands as a commitment to one's pledging their moral and physical support toward that leader and the cause. By the placing of their hands over the prophet Muhammad's, and/or his successor(s), they are literally binding their trust and allegiance with Allah. The highest level of bonding for the radical Islamist and for all Muslims is that of their allegiance with Allah. This historical tribal and religious tradition is confirmed and praised by Allah in the following quote from the Holy Qur'an:

> **Allah's Good Pleasure was on the believers when they swore Fealty to the (Muhammad) under tree. He knew what was in their hearts, and He send down tranquility to them; and He rewarded them with a speedy victory. And many gains will they acquire.** (48:18&19)

This revelation has a significant influence on the present day radical Islamist and their religious-based ideology, for Allah has promised them a **"speedy victory"** in return for their dedicated and undeniable allegiance to Him and to Muhammad. For the present radical Islamist this belief was proven by the numerous historically recorded victories experienced by Muhammad and his successors in the seventh through the eleventh centuries, with the establishment of the Islamic Empire marked as their "Golden Age." One must remember that when the Islamic Empire was experiencing their "Golden Age," Europe was deeply into their "Dark Ages." However, in the twentieth century the Islamic Mujahidin once again experienced victory in the 1979 war and the fall of the Soviet Union. It was the 1979 victory that proved to the radical Islamists that Allah was once again in their favor and that as long as they were committed to and pledge their undeniable allegiance to Allah as his warriors that they could do no wrong for now they were fulfilling the will of Allah. Their acts of violence became symbolic because they were fighting for the *"Purification of the Soul of Islam."* Islamic history has recorded that the seventh century warriors were triumphant in all of their battles because they remained loyal and committed to Allah and Muhammad. Surat 48, verse 29, confirms this belief for the radical Islamist: ***"Muhammad is the Messenger of Allah, and those who are with him are strong against Unbelievers, but compassionate amongst each other."*** The Qur'an not only dictates what the young converts must do but it also makes it obligatory for all Muslims to pledge their allegiance to Muhammad in order to prove their devout trust and faith in Allah. ***"And whoever has not believed in Allah and His Messenger—then indeed, We have prepared for the disbelievers a Blaze"*** (48:15). It is this belief in the power of being loyal and undeniably committed to Allah and to Muhammad that confirms their ideology for *"**to Allah belong the forces (soldiers) of the heavens and the earth. And Allah Exalted in Power and full of wisdom"*** (48:4 & 7).

Historical pride plus their unconditional belief in the revelations of Allah and the words of Muhammad have played a major role in the development of issues which are still haunting the radical Islamist movement of the twenty-first century. In order to entice these young Muslims to violence, the ideology must first place a sense of moral outrage into the thinking and beliefs of their followers. Therefore, the content of the violations must justify the individual's personal rage and anger and their strong desire and belief that they have been chosen by Allah to erase the shame and restore the pure soul of Islam. This moral ideology is built on the strong belief that the world has decayed into a morass of greed and moral depravity and therefore it instills within these fighters that they are heroes, for they are fighting for justice and fairness for all Muslims throughout the world. Therefore their actions must be of symbolic nature in order to become role models for their young recruits.

Remember that ideology is a set of beliefs and ideas that are shared by a group that not only have the power to influence but also the power to motivate various behaviors and attitudes. In other words, it is this ideology that is based on the historical religious pride and prejudice of the leaders of the revival of the radical Islamist that dictates their conscious and unconscious habits and mind-set. By incorporating an ideology based on religion, the religious leaders of the radical Islamist movement have been able to inspire and incite both the Muslim youth and the Muslim masses worldwide to attack those individuals and institutions which are perceived to be the *enemies of Islam*. For the radical Islamist, the world is divided into *Dar-al-Islam*, a geographical region in which Islam is the dominate religion and it is ruled only by the Shari'ah law, which literally means the *"abode of Islam,"* and *Dar-al-Harb*, a geographical region which has not submitted to Islam and the

Shari'ah law and is therefore automatically considered to be at war with Islam, which literally means the *"abode of war."* For the radical Islamist you are either a *believer* or a *nonbeliever* and you either adhere to Shari'ah law or you do not. There is no middle ground; it is either or. They believe that Islam is the only religion to rule the world and that they *"are the best nation ever to be produced before mankind. You enjoin the right, forbid the wrong, and believe in Allah"* (3:31). I must add here that in both the Qur'an and the Hadith the words *Dar-al- Islam* and/or *Dar al-Harb* are not found, but what is found is the concept that the world is divided into believers and nonbelievers, or good versus evil. However, the doctrine that divided the world between *Dar-al-Islam* and *Dar-al-Harb* (believers versus nonbelievers) is found in the literary work of Al-Shaheed Sayyid Qutb, who is recognized as one of the grandfathers of the present day Jihad movement, one of the late leaders of the Muslim Brotherhood multinational organization, and author of one of the most famous and printed radical Islamist books, *Milestones Along the Road* (*Ma'alim fi al-T of ariq*). For example, in Surat 4, verse 76, Allah informs his followers that, *"Those who believe fight in the cause of Allah and those who reject faith fight in the cause of Evil (tagut): so fight ye against the friends of Satan—feeble deed is the cunning Satan."* And in verse 73 of Surat 9 Allah reveals to Muhammad: *"O Prophet strive hard against the Unbelievers and the Hypocrites and be firm against them. Their abode is Hell, an evil refuge indeed."* In these two revelations Allah makes it clear how the unbelievers are to be treated but He also places the distinction that Muhammad is an example and a role model of how these unbelievers are to be treated. Throughout the Qur'an, the radical Islamists have noted revelation after revelation that gives distinction and exemplifies their symbolic acts of terror.

In creating their ideology and quest to *"purify the soul of Islam"* they have capitalized on the Islamic community that originated in the seventh century and the devout Muslim veterans who either served and/or supported the guerilla warfare Jihad under the leadership of Muhammad. I apologize for repeating this message numerous times throughout this chapter but it is one important factor that so many individuals, including many within the American government, have chosen to ignore and/or deny or both. Why? I have not comprehended this, especially since for radical Islamists and the Muslim's ummah their Islamic history is very important as it reveals Allah's purpose for all mankind. They are bound by a code of honor that they have inherited from ancient times and that is relearned by each generation. Islam permeates every aspect of society; therefore, it must be thought of as a religion and as a social order that is dictated by the revelations of God and rooted in their sacred texts and enforced by the Shari'ah law (Islamic law). It is their historical pride that plays a major role in the development of issues, which are still haunting the radical Islamist movement of the twenty-first century.

Graham Fuller, a scholar specializing in Islam and Arab politics, asked the following question: "Does political Islam represent the last heroic stand of Muslim cultural resistance to galloping globalization with an American accent?" **(2)** I agree that the present day radical Islamists and their call for a Global Jihad do represent a heroic stand of the Muslim cultural resistance but I question if it is their last stand. Only time will tell! One must remember that prior to the Hijrah Muhammad was a religious missionary seeking only converts in Mecca and the term Jihad referred to an individual's struggle within oneself in regard to his or her sin(s). However, after his emigration to Medina and

Allah's new revelations to fight the enemies of Islam, Jihad became a movement to conquer territory and fight against the "enemies of Islam." A note of reminder: all revelations received by Muhammad after his emigration to Medina, in 622 AD, **abrogate or replace all previous revelations he received while a missionary in Mecca**. Review section 12 in chapter II, "The Hijrah, The Soul of Islam." By emulating the actions and mind-set of their early ancestors and their role model Muhammad, the twenty-first century mujahidin believe they are enforcing justice as obligated by Allah's revelations. It is because of this belief that radical Islamists and the Muslim masses worldwide are inspired to attack those individuals and institutions which are perceived to be the "enemies of Islam."

It is this generation of Islamic mujahidin who believe they have been endowed by Allah and Muhammad to continue the quest of the seventh century to make all mankind come under the only religion of the world - Islam. Narrated by Abu Huraira: Allah's Apostle (Muhammad, peace be upon him) said, "I have been sent with the shortest expressions bearing the widest meanings, and I have been made victorious with terror (cast in the hearts of the enemy), and while I was sleeping, the keys of the treasures of the world were brought to me and put in my hand." Abu Huraira added: "Allah's Apostle (Muhammad) has left the world and now you, people, are bringing out those treasures" (i.e. the Prophet did not benefit by them). **(3)** For the radical Islamist, it is their historical Islamic roots that are dictating their beliefs, their ideology, and their symbolic violence.

NOTES:

1. Bukhari, Hadith, Volume 9, Book 88, Number 178, narrated by Junada bin Abi Umaiya. Ttps://www.sahih-bukhari.com/Pages/Bukhari_9_88.php.(Retrieved 3/27/2017)

2. Graham Fuller, "The Future of Political Islam, Introduction", Palgrave/Macmillan, 2003. P.V.

3. Sahih Bukhari Volume4, Book52, Number 220, Narrated by Abu Huraira. http://quranx.com/(Hadith/Bukhari/USC-MSA/Volume-4/Book-52/Hadith-220/ (Retrieved 3/1/2/2017)

IV
FIGHTING FOR THE SOUL OF ISLAM:
GLOBAL JIHAD

"God's principles and doctrine of war"
"Our youth are different from your soldiers. Your problem will be how to convince your troops to fight, while our problem will be how to restrain our youths." **(1)**

"Allah is our objective. The Prophet is our leader. Qur'an is our law. Jihad is our way. Dying in the way of Allah is our highest hope."
—Motto of the Muslim Brotherhood & the Radical Islamist

For the radical Islamist, Jihad is an intrinsic part of Islam. It is a religious struggle, a struggle between good and evil. The Islamic faith is a total way of life, from birth to death, and to speak of the

Islamic ummah one is referring to all Muslims of all nationalities in all nations of this world. As revealed in the previous chapter, the radical Islamists ideology is defined by their beliefs and ideas and their quest to be the best nation ever to be produced by mankind as promised within the Holy Qur'an, Surat 3:104 and 110: *"And let there be [arising] from you a nation inviting to [all that is] good, enjoining what is right and forbidding what is wrong, and those will be the successful" (3:104)* and *"You are the best nation ever to be produced before mankind. You enjoin the right, forbid the wrong, and believe in Allah." (3:110)*. It is because of this driven need to be the *"best nation ever"* that the twenty-first century Jihadist has called for the purification of the soul of Islam, which in actuality is the fundamental Islamic tradition of revival (tajdid) and renewal (islah). Roots to both of these traditions can be traced to two Islamic sacred texts, the Holy Qur'an and the Sunnah/Hadith. It is very important for one to understand that *tijded* or revival is based on a tradition that was set forth by the Prophet Muhammad in the seventh century in which he declared that, "Allah shall raise for this Ummah at the head of every century a man who shall renew (or revive) for it its religion." **(2)** This "man who shall renew (or revive) Islam for it is religion" will be known as *"Mujahid"* **(reviver or *Deen*) the merciful servant of the ummah**. He will fear no one but Allah, revive and renew the soul of Islam, and tolerate no opposition to the Shari'ah law. This merciful servant may be a Caliph, a prominent Imam (teacher), an influential devout Muslim, or a saint *(wali)*. **By the Islamic calendar, November 1979 marked the beginning of the fifteenth century and Muslims throughout the world celebrated with hope and expectation of a new *Mujahid* who would revive the global Islamic community.** A number of key historical events marked the beginning of a revival and renewal to their faith, their

Islamic communities, and the radical extremist: **(1)** the Iranian Revolution in 1979, in which many Shiite believed that the charismatic leader Ayatollah Khomeini was the Mujahid that the Prophet Muhammad had promised; **(2)** the Egyptian-Israel peace treaty, signed by Egyptian President Anwar Sadat, the United States President Jimmy Carter, and the Prime Minister of Israel Menachen Begin. (The Muslim Brotherhood and other Islamic extremists were angered that President Sadat had recognized Israel as a nation and had formed a peace treaty with Allah's enemy, Israel. Three years later Anwar Sadat was brutally murdered by Islamic extremists from the Egyptian Military, because of his part in the peace treaty); and **(3)** the Soviet Union invasion of Afghanistan that led to the fall of the Soviet Union by the Islamic mujahidin and the formation of the largest and first non-national terrorist organization: al-Qaeda and its charismatic leader bin Laden. Many Sunni youth and extremist Muslims believed him to be the promised *Mujahid.* These three events in the new fifteenth Islamic calendar century did in fact reshape the Middle East, revive Islamic resurgence movements, and revive and renew the fighting for the soul of the Muslim global ummah—revival *(tajdid)* and renewal *(islah).* Young Muslims, from around the world, are willing to leave their families, homes, communities, and their nations to sacrifice their lives for Allah; to continue the battle started by Muhammad and his early followers, who invaded tribes, cities, and territories; to spread the message of Allah; and to convert the masses to Islam. It is because of their heritage, beliefs, and commitment that I refer to them as *"warriors of Allah—God."*

For the Islamic Jihadist, the legitimacy and justification for their ideology, their call for a Global Jihad, and their horrendous acts of violence are found within two sacred texts, the first being the Holy Qur'an, the true and pure revelations of Allah, and the second being the Sunnah/Hadith, the sayings and deeds of Muhammad, the last messenger of Allah as recorded by his companions. Both of these texts, as interpreted by the radical Islamist and many Muslims, are a call for all true believers to return to the fundamentals of Islam. Many individuals do not want to hear that the Qur'an commands war and to fight the infidels with strength and vigor. One must remember that Islam survived and spread in the environment of armed violence; therefore, it is the goal and vision of the present-day warriors of Allah to continue the fighting and the spreading of the Islamic faith until the entire world is converted under Shari'ah law and/ or the end of the world. Some may question my above statement that the mujahidin will "continue the fighting and spreading of the Islamic faith until the entire world is under Shari'ah law," or the end of the world. But that is exactly what bin Laden and the other Islamic leaders have professed, as they believe they are directed by Allah and Allah only. I confirm my statement based on various statements made by the radical Islamist leaders and the revelation found in Surat 33:27 that Allah ***"made you (warriors of Allah) heirs of their lands, their houses, and their goods, and of a land which ye had not frequented (before). And Allah has Power over all things."*** In order to establish why they do what they do, one must have both an understanding and knowledge of their specific beliefs and their interpretations of both of these two sacred texts. Both of these sources have such an historical presence that defines not only their identity as **warriors of God** but also distinguishes them as devout believers. Jihad for the radical Islamist is the revival *(tajdid)*, the renewal *(islah)*, and the spreading *(aintishar)* of their faith throughout the world as commanded by Allah and exemplified by Muhammad.

The first source, and the most revered of texts within a Muslim's life, is found within the principles and doctrine as recorded within the Holy Qur'an for all mankind. In Arabic the word "**al**" means "*the*" and "**lah**" means "*God*," hence "*The God*" or "*Allah*". It was through these revelations that Allah advised and encouraged Muhammad on how to fight and how to declare war against all nonbelievers (*Kufr*) and it is also through these same revelations that young Muslim men define who they are and how to fight for Allah's cause. Michael Rack, in his book *From Muhammad to Burj Khalifa,* stated: "*The Qur'an is the literal word of God that existed in its entirety for all eternity*" **(3).** For centuries, the Qur'an has defined every aspect of a Muslim's daily life, from praying for guidance the food he/she can eat to their relationships, and even how to be Mujahid *for Allah*. The Holy Qur'an was explained to me as being the purest voice of Allah. It was not written by Muhammad, but rather it was revealed to him through a series of revelations from Allah over a period of twenty-three years. Surat 39:1 & 2, answer two very important questions asked by many about Allah and the power found not only within His revelations but also in the lives and actions of many Muslims. The first verse answers the question as to Allah's power in sending His revelations to man: **"The revelation of this Book is from Allah, the exalted in Power, full of wisdom"** and the second verse answers the question as to why true wisdom is found in carrying out Allah's will for "**Verily, it is We Who have revealed the Book to thee, in Truth: so serve Allah, offering Him sincere devotion."** The pure attributes of Allah are defined in numerous Surat's found within the Holy Qur'an but the one which I have found to be the most beautiful is Surat 59:22-24:

Allah is He, than Whom there is no other god;
Who knows (all things) both secret and open; He,
Most Gracious, Most Merciful. (23) Allah is He,
than Whom there is no other god. The Sovereign,
The Holy One, The Source (and perfection), The
Guardian of Faith, The Preserver of Safety, The
Exalted in Might, The Irresistible, the justly Proud
Glory to Allah! (High is He) Above the part-
ners they attribute to Him. (24) He is Allah, The
Creator, The Originator, The Fashioner, To Him
belong the Most Beautiful Names: Whatever is
in the Heavens and on earth, doth declare His
Praise and Glory and He is the Exalted in Might,
the Wise.

Three very important points are made in the above three verses: **first**, Allah created the world and all aspects of it to total perfection for the Muslims and **secondly**, that Allah is the most sovereign God above all else in this world. Allah declares His supremacy over the entire world and describes himself Allâh! *Lâ ilâha illa Huwa* (none has the right to be worshipped but Allah). When Allah speaks it is so! And **thirdly**, as found within the Qur'an, the Torah, and the Bible, God defines His supremacy and the only purpose for which He created mankind is to *worship Him* and to Him alone belongs whatever is in Heaven and whatever is on earth. It is within these three verses that the pure sovereignty of Allah is established, and therefore for Muslims Islam can be **the only true religion**—"Allah Akbar." The Prophet, peace be Upon him, said, "The keys of the unseen are five and none knows them but Allah: **(a)** None knows what is in the womb, but Allah: **(b)** None knows what will happen tomorrow, but Allah; **(c)** None knows when it will rain, but

Allah; **(d)** None knows where he will die, but Allah (knows that); and none knows when the Hour will be established, but Allah" **(4)**. All Muslims believe that they will be held accountable by God in their next life for all and any choices they may make during their life here on earth. What one must remember is that **the Qur'an is the foremost communicator for the twenty-first century Global Jihads, as it defines for them their self-esteem and their self-identity. The Qur'an is the ending source of all divine inspiration for all devout Muslims.** The following guideline will assist you in becoming familiar with the Holy Qur'an and assist you in understanding and comprehending why and how the Qur'an has been the dominate driving source for the twenty-first century radical Islamist. The Qur'an contains more than 109 verses that the radical Islamist has claimed is calling them to war—a sacred war against all nonbelievers, *Kufr,* whether they are Muslim or non-Muslim. **Guideline #1,** for all Muslims, the Holy Qur'an is the final and only divine will of Allah, written as a book of guidance for all mankind throughout the entire world no matter what a man's color, race, and/or nationality may be. **It is the foremost sacred of books and therefore the whole human race must adhere to and believe in its commands as set forth by Allah. Guideline #2,** in reading and studying various verses found within the Holy Qur'an one quickly learns that they are what in literary studies are termed "open-ended texts." In other words they are not restrained by definite limits or by the historical context of surrounding text, and therefore they allow for a spontaneous response such as we have noted with al-Qaeda, ISIS, and other radical Islamist movements. I learned this very important factor during my studies of the Qur'an and the historical context to the passages of scripture surrounding that text. **Guideline #3,** for Muslims, the Qur'an is only the pure, true, and legal revelations of Allah if it is written only in Arabic and printed by the King Fahd Holy Qur'an complex in Mecca, Saudi Arabia. All Quranic verses quoted within this chapter and book have been taken from the Holy Qur'an edited by the Presidency of Islamic Researches, IFTA, and printed by the King Fahd Holy Qur'an complex in Mecca, Saudi Arabia. I have noted which Surat (Chapter) I have taken my quotes from as well as the verse(s). For example, Surat 8, verse 24, will be noted as 8:24. Not only must the Qur'an be written in Arabic to be authentic but it also must be recited in the original language that it was revealed to Muhammad by the Angel Gabriel - Arabic. Any other language is considered to be merely a translation and therefore not the divine words of Allah. During my teaching and lecturing I have experienced Muslims, from a wide variety of nationalities, reciting verses from the Qur'an in Arabic and yet, a number of them, when asked to please translate what they had recited for their fellow participants, had no understanding because they did not speak Arabic. I was quickly informed that they had been taught to recite the verses in Arabic during their religious classes at their local Mosque but they had not been taught the translation. In Surat 17:106 Allah informs Muslims that **"We have revealed this Qur'an little by little so that you may recite it to people at intervals, and We have revealed it gradually."** Note that the proper spelling of this Holy book is Qur'an not Koran, as there is no 'K' in the Arabic Alphabet. **Guideline # 4:** the chapters (Surat's in Arabic) in the Qur'an are not recorded in chronological order, the order in which Muhammad received the sacred revelations from Allah, but rather by their individual length. For example according to religious scholars the first revelation revealed to Muhammad by the angel Gabriel is actually the first verse found within Surat 96 (*Al-Alaq*). **"Recite in the name of your Lord who created man from a clinging** *substance. Who taught by the pen—taught man that which he knew not?"* (96:1-5) Therefore, one will note that the shorter revelations are found in the beginning of the Qur'an and proceed to the longest chapter. This is confusing to many non-Muslim readers who assume that the Qur'an is recorded the same as the Christian Bible and/or the Jewish Torah. However, guideline number 4 is very helpful in assisting individuals in comprehending the descriptions and accounts of the radical Islamist movement, ideology, brutality, and commitments to becoming warriors of Allah as noted within this chapter and book. **Guideline # 5** is the *law of abrogation or Naskh* in Arabic, which means lifting and removing. During my concentrated studies I learned that Allah revealed various signs, miracles, and revelations to Muhammad that were to supersede all previous revelations, miracles, and signs. Allah's acknowledgement and justification for abrogation is found within Surat 2:106: **"None of Our revelations do we abrogate or cause to be forgotten, but We substitute something better or similar: Knowest thou not that Allah Hath power over all things?"** and can also be found within 3:39, 16:101, and 7:86. This can further be explained by becoming aware that the Qur'an is divided into two prominent periods, called the *Meccan* period and the *Medinan* period. These two periods are defined by the life of Muhammad as the last Prophet and the development of the Islamic ummah over a period of twenty-three years. During the first period of Muhammad's life, referred to as the *Meccan* period, he was calling the people of Mecca to become part of the new Islamic faith. It is in the revelations recorded during this period that one notes poetic verses that speak of mercy, compassion, kindness, and *"no compulsion in religion,"* as found in Surat 2:246 and 2:256 & 257. However, it is during the latter part of Muhammad's life, or the second period, the

Medinan period, that the prophet and his converts were fleeing for their lives that Allah ordered him to wage war against all nonbelievers: *"If anyone desires a religion other than Islam (submission to God), never will it be accepted of him; and in the Hereafter he will be in the ranks of those who have lost (All spiritual good)."* Surat 3:85 abrogates, or eliminates, 2:246, 2:256 & 257. For Muslims, the abrogating of previous revelations speaking of tolerance and peace from the *Meccan* period, by the later revelations speaking of war against all evil as found within the *Medinan* period, is not a contradiction but rather Allah improving His messages to His devout followers. Surat 13:39 states that *"Allah doth blot out or confirm what He pleaseth: with Him is the Mother of the Book."* Guideline #6: Allah informs all Muslims what they can expect upon their death. Death and one's life in the hereafter is very prominent on all Muslims' minds and Allah in the Holy Qur'an makes it very clear that He and He alone makes the final decisions of their fate. Allah, reveals the various levels of the *Gardens of Paradise* and informs His devout believers that the greatest sacrifice one can make is fighting for His Cause. Hence the present day ample quantity of young followers who are dedicated to becoming martyrs, willing to die for the cause of Allah. Each of the above noted guidelines provide a stepping-stone to the understanding of why the radical Islamists do what they do and why and how they justify all of their actions and beliefs using the Holy Qur'an.

The second most sacred and revered source that Muslims are to pattern their lives after is found within the sayings and deeds of the Prophet Muhammad as recorded in the **Sunnah/Hadith**. Unlike the Qur'an, the *Sunnah/Hadith* was never edited and placed in one documented text but rather it is a collection of his teachings and his actions upon which the moral roots and structure of Islam are founded. These individually recorded collections are called **Sunna** (Sunnah), which in Arabic means **tradition**. Al-Qaeda, ISIS, and members of the al-Qaeda (base) network are "**Sunni Muslims**" and often refer to themselves as the pure "**traditional Muslims**" and therefore consider themselves to be more devout and pure Muslims than the Shiite Muslims, which in Arabic means "*the Party of Ali.*" It is this belief that has caused centuries of resentment, hatred, distrust, and brutal fighting between the Sunni and the Shiite Muslims since 632 AD. It is a battle fueled by generations of hatred and resentment that the radical Islamists, in the twenty-first century, still use to justify their brutality and the horrendous act of violence used against each other. Muhammad has prominence in both the Sunni and the Shiite Islamic sects for it is Allah who clarified the prominence of Muhammad for all Muslins throughout the world when He stated: *"**Muhammad is not the father of any of your men, but (he is) The Messenger of Allah, and the Seal of the Prophets; and Allah has full knowledge of all things**"*(33:40). In this verse Allah has commanded Muhammad with the mission of not only being His last messenger but also He has chosen him to be the one to receive His revelations and to represent the divine link between Himself and man. For Muslims around the world, Muhammad closed the line of messengers chosen by Allah and he is therefore referred to as the last Prophet. Not only did Allah designate Muhammad as His Messenger but He also gave Muhammad His *"Seal of the Prophets,"* which signifies that this is Allah's final and complete decision and therefore no additions or substitutions can be made **(5).** For the radical Islamist, Muhammad has been ordained by Allah as the last Prophet for the world, not just for the Muslims but for all mankind. Allah's Apostle Muhammad, peace be upon him, said: "I have been ordered (by Allah) to fight against the people until they testify that none has the right to be worshipped but Allah and that Muhammad is Allah's Apostle, and offer the prayers perfectly and give the obligatory charity, so if they perform at that, then they save their lives and property from me except for Islamic laws and then their reckoning (accounts) will be done by Allah" **(6).** My studies in Islamic thought (*madhahib*) and the Sunnah/Hadith was concentrated on the Sahih al-Bukhari school, which is recognized by the Wahabi, *Al-Wahhābīyya,* the Sunni, and the Shiite as one of the three most respected and, accurate translations of the sacred sayings and life of the Prophet Muhammad. Therefore, the references to the Sunnah/Hadith made throughout this chapter are taken from his volumes. Because Allah revealed His revelations on war and the destruction of all nonbelievers in the later part of Muhammad's life, the *Medinan* Period, the **law of abrogating** is also found within the sacred text of the Sunnah/Hadith. As circumstances changed within the Muslim ummah so did Muhammad's teachings and messages to his followers. For example, the following quote in reference to the direction in which all Muslims must face when performing their daily *Salah* prayers:

> The Prophet prayed facing *Bait-ul-Maqdis* (i.e. Jerusalem) for sixteen or seventeen months but he wished that his *Qibla* would be the *Ka'ba* (at Mecca). (So Allah Revealed (2.144) and he offered 'As prayers (in his Mosque facing Ka'ba at Mecca) and some people prayed with him. A man from among those who had prayed with him went out and passed by some people offering prayer in another mosque, and they were in the state of bowing. He said, "I, (swearing by Allah,)

testify that I have prayed with the Prophet facing Mecca." Hearing that, they turned their faces to the Ka'ba while they were still bowing. Some men had died before the *Qibla* was changed towards the *Ka'ba*. They had been killed and we did not know what to say about them (i.e. whether their prayers towards Jerusalem were accepted or not). So Allah revealed: *"And Allah would never make your faith (i.e. prayer) to be lost (i.e. your prayers offered (towards Jerusalem." Truly Allah is Full of Pity, Most Merciful towards mankind." (2.143) (7)*

Like Muhammad, and his devoted followers, today's Jihadist are dedicated to do whatever it takes to establish a global Muslim ummah of pure and true believers who are committed and willing to make the ultimate sacrifice for Allah and for Islam. The thirteenth century Persian Islamic scholar and poet Jalāl ad-Dīn Muhammad Rūmi made numerous documented statements about the Prophet: "Be among the community (of believers) who are blessed by (Divine) Mercy. Don't abandon the way of conduct of Muhammad," **(8)** "He brings all of those (who are) led astray into the Way out of the desert. May Muhammad be the guide on the Way of God forever?" **(9)** Allah in Surat 4:80 established Muhammad as His guardian over all Muslims: *"He obeys the Messenger, obeys Allah: but if any turns away, We have not sent thee to watch over them."*

Jihad is not one of the five religious pillars of Islam, as bin Laden and other radical Islamist leaders have tried to claim. Their reasoning is that like the five religious pillars, Jihad was made mandatory by Allah in His last revelations, such as in Surat 9. In the Holy Quran,

Surat 22:78, and in the sacred Hadith, the five pillars are defined to be the foundation of all Muslims' lives. Muhammad, peace be upon him, said: "Islam is based on (the following) five (principles): 1. To testify that none has the right to be worshipped but Allah and Muhammad is Allah's Apostle. 2. To offer the (compulsory congregational) prayers dutifully and perfectly. 3. To pay Zakat (i.e. obligatory charity). 4. To perform Hajj. (I.e. Pilgrimage to Mecca) 5. To observe fast during the month of Ramadan" **(10).** As there are no national boundaries attached to these five pillars they are recognized and followed by all Muslims throughout the world. The word *Jihad*, in Arabic, literally means *striving* or *struggling,* and within the Qur'an Allah defines that there are two types of *striving* or *struggling* which all human beings must endure—a *"Greater Jihad"* and a *"Lesser Jihad."*

The Greater Jihad (*al-Jihad al-Akbar)* is a nonviolent Jihad, in which an individual struggles with Satan between *good and evil.* The enemy, Satan, is unseen, and therefore it is an internal spiritual warfare that man must face daily. It is purely a spiritual striving, one which must be undertaken *"with sincerity and under discipline"* as revealed in Surat 22:78 of the Holy Qur'an:

> *And strive (jihidu) in His cause as ye ought to strive, (with sincerity and under discipline). He has chosen you, and has imposed no difficulties on you. In religion; it is the religion of your father Abraham. It is He who has named you Muslims, both before and in this (Revelation). That the Messenger may be a witness for you, and ye be witnesses for mankind! So establish regular Prayer, give zakat, and hold fast to Allah!*

He is your Protector – The best to protect and the best to help!

The Christian concept of original sin does not and has not ever existed within the Islamic faith. Ibn Abi al-Dunya, a ninth century Islamic traditionalist, wrote and taught moral self-examination, in which Muslims are to practice self-denial as a spiritual discipline as *"one fights with one's own soul"* in an internal spiritual warfare between good and evil. I especially remember how much I enjoyed reading his book *Holding the Soul Accountable and Blaming It (Muhhasibat al-nafs wa-l-izra 'alayha)*, in which various doctrines on moral examinations and the individual's soul were discussed. I learned that it was Ibn Abi al-Dunya's doctrines that became part of the Sufi teachings. The *Greater Jihad* is a moral warfare in which one is to strive for a closer and intimate relationship with Allah.

The second type of Jihad found within the Islamic faith and commanded by Allah is called the *Lesser Jihad (al-Jihad al-asghar)*. Unlike the *Greater Jihad*, which is an internal struggle between good and bad the *Lesser Jihad* is an external struggle, a war, declared by Allah against all *Kufr*—nonbelievers—*"**Wherever you find them.**"* This chapter is devoted to the external struggle in which the universal Muslim ummah is commanded to fight to conquer and purify the soul of Islam. The radical Islamists have no misconception of what the external struggle is or who is the external enemy, those who believe in Allah and his revelations and those who do not. It is Allah's call for a universal brotherhood and Muhammad's years as a warrior that explain one of the key elements of their behavior. It is these two sacred Islamic sources that are the leading factors that must be understood and accepted if one is to comprehend *why they do what they do.* It is Muhammad's role as a *warrior of Allah* plus the various revelations, such as Surat 22:39 & 40 in the Qur'an, that the radical Islamists believe they have been commanded to both declare war and to judge all nonbelievers in the name of Allah. For *"did not Allah check one set of people by means of another,"* and did He not promise them that "*Allah will certainly aid those who aid His cause."* But Allah also in verse 40 establishes His supremacy, *"for verily Allah is full of Strength, Exalted in Might (Able to enforce His Will)."* Allah's words are supreme and therefore cannot be questioned or deviated from. It is in these two verses that the radical Islamists have interpreted that they no longer need to fight only in a defensive war, for Allah has now commanded them to fight in an aggressive offensive war—**A Just Cause War**. Once again, the *"law of abrogation"* applies to these two verses as they were revealed to Muhammad during the *Medinan* period.

In the previous listings of the six major guidelines for reading and understanding the Qur'an I discussed in Guideline #5 the *"law of abrogation."* How does this *"law of abrogation"* impact and enable the radical Islamist to declare and justify their fight in a global Jihad against all non-Muslims? Extremely, for it supports and validates their carnage and their call for a worldwide Jihad. On numerous occasions I have witnessed how many individuals, including members of the international diplomatic corps, and especially citizens and governments of non-Muslim countries, do not understand the importance or the impact that the *"law of abrogation"* plays in Islamic theology. For example, statements such as *"there is no compulsion in religion"* or that *"Jihad is only an internal struggle and not a call for war"* reveal just how numerous uninformed individuals lack any real comprehension of how influential the *"law of abrogation"* truly is to the radical Islamist and many devout Muslims. The *"law of abrogation"* is found within various Quranic Surat's (chapters) but none is more distinct in defining the pure nature of Jihad and Allah's commands on how to fight the world's nonbelievers than that of Surat 9, titled *"Repentance"* (*Al-Tauba*). It is recorded as being the last revelation revealed to Muhammad and therefore it abrogates, or nullifies, all previous recorded revelations. Historically it is placed about 631 AD, around the time that Muhammad led his expedition against the Byzantine Empire. Surat 9 is often referred to by Muslim scholars as the *"Surat of war,"* and/or as the *"Surat of Punishment"* because it reveals how the warriors of Allah are to fight and how they are to punish all the nonbelievers. Abu Bakr, the first Caliph following Muhammad's death and Muhammad's closest friend, used Surat 9 as his validation to continue the Prophet's fighting to conquer new converts and new territory. ISIS's newly self-proclaimed Caliph, Abu Bakr al-Baghdadi, in his Friday sermons and in many of ISIS's international press releases, quotes regularly from Surat 9 in validating their acts of brutality and terror. This is not a coincidence, as al-Baghdadi not only chose Abu Bakr as his Caliph name but he has also incorporated the first Caliph's war strategies and savagery as found in Surat 9. ISIS uses the *"law of abrogation"* and Surat 9 as both their justification and their road map for their acts of carnage and inhumane violence. Like Abu Bakr, al-Baghdadi, and bin Laden, the present day radical Islamists also adhere to and fully accept the sayings and deeds of Muhammad during the Medinan period (war period). Because Surat 9 is the *"Surat of war"* it is the only Surat out of the 114 found within the Holy Qur'an that does not begin with the *Bismilliah ar-Rahan ar-Rahim*—which states **"In the name of Allah, the compassionate, the merciful."** Bismilliah was a cry for help and security from Allah and is the first phrase taught to children in Quranic recitation and in Islamic schools. According to the *"laws of abrogation"* and the verses found within Surat 9 the radical Islamists are not terrorists but rather **warriors of Allah,** and their brutal and horrendous acts of violence are sanctioned by Allah and therefore they are fighting a *"just war."* In the following paragraphs I shall endeavor to discuss and explain why I believe that Surat 9 is one of the most influential Surat's for the twenty-first century radical Islamist movement and how and why the *"laws of abrogation"* need to be acknowledged within our nation's strategies for counter/terrorism security. In this one Surat, Allah has given fifteen significant and influential commands that the radical Islamists believe gives them permission to declare war against all nonbelievers *"where ever they find them"*: (1) Allah's total "sovereignty," **la ilaha illa allah** (There is no deity except God); (2) **there is to be no religion in the world but Islam,** for it is the only *"true religion"* **and therefore all mankind must submit to its authority: (3)** the pure nature of Jihad *"kill all nonbelievers where you may find them"*; (4) the world is divided between good (*Dar-al-Islam*) versus evil (*Dar-al-Harb*); (5) there are to be no geographical boundaries in Islam—hence a global Jihad; (6) Islam is both a religion and a political movement—there is to be no separation between church and state; (7) Jihad is a holy duty made obligatory upon all Muslims by Allah, the Almighty; (8) all previous contracts and treaties for peace are null and void; (9) defines who are the believers—*"the truthful ones"*; (10) the dominance of Muslims over Christians and Jews; (11) the aggressiveness in which the warriors of Allah are to fight all nonbelievers; (12) *"now"* they are given permission to fight an offensive warfare to conquer and spread Islam throughout the world; (13) the young Mujahid are commanded to make the ultimate sacrifice—become martyrs, *Shaheed,* for Allah;

(14) that Jihad be declared against all **"polytheists and the hypocrites and that they be treated harshly"**; and (15) one of the most significant for our nation's national security and counter/terrorism strategies found within Surat 9 is that it describes the profile of the potential radical Islamic recruit. David Cook describes Surat 9 as "the revocation of the immunity granted by God and Muhammad to those tribes that had not converted to Islam prior to the revelation. After the lifting of immunity, the Muslims must fight the unbelievers" **(11).** Each of these listed fifteen commands is paramount in understanding the radical Islamist mind-set and why they do what they do; therefore, as justification of my personal conclusions I have quoted from the sacred text of both the Holy Qur'an and the Sunnah/Hadith.

I had originally critiqued each verse in Surat 9 to justify my personal interpretation of the radical Islamists behavior, mind-set and violence that defines **why they do what they do;** however, upon noting both the length and the redundancy of such a breakdown I decided to elaborate on the following key verses which define the previous noted fifteen significant and influential commands found within Surat: (1) **"verse of the Sword"** (9:5); (2) **"Allah will punish them by your hands"**(9:14 and 15), (3) the "sovereignty of Allah" (9:16); the (4) **"Islam is the true religion"** and **"dominance of Muslims over Jews and Christians"**(9:29); (5) **"obligation to fight in Allah's cause"** (9:38; 39); (6) **"the ultimate sacrifice"**—Martyrdom (9:38,39,41and 111), (7) **"apostasy in Islam is worse than being an infidel"** (9:66, 73, 74 and 77); the (8) **"Salvific (leading to salvation) covenant"** (9:111); (9) **"aggressiveness and harshness to be shown to the nonbelievers"**(9:1-6, 14-16, 73- 74 and 123).

The first inflectional command and the one most quoted by the international media and various prominent Jihadists is the *"verse of the sword"* (9:5): *"fight and slay them, and seize them, beleaguer them, and lie in wait for them in every stratagem of war."* In this one verse Allah has commanded His Mujahid what He requires of them as His warriors. They are commanded to use aggression to *"lie in wait for them"* (the nonbelievers) and to use *"every stratagem of war"* (deception, mass killings, decapitation, crucifixion, and other forms of brutality) for they are fighting a *"just war,"* a war called for by Allah, and they are fighting for Allah's cause. The *"verse of the sword"* (9:5) is the one verse in all of the Holy Qur'an that *abrogates* at least 120 previous revelation verses **(12).** No example is more prominent throughout the world of the power and influence of Surat 9:5 than the attack on 9/11. Following Allah's command as found in 9:5 bin Laden gave the US a period of grace to repent from their sinful ways, *"But when the forbidden months are past, then fight and slay the Pagans wherever ye find them, and seize them."* An when our nation did not respond favorably, hence the 9/11 attack, in which 2,996 people were killed and over 6,000 were injured. Shame and dishonor is a powerful motivator in the Arab/Islamic culture and is the leading factor as to why I stated in the previous chapter that I was not surprised by the 9/11 attacks. In order to save face, prevent shame, and to retain his status, honor, and position as the leader of al-Qaeda, bin Laden had to follow up his declaration of war by attacking the United States. But his attack could not be just any attack, it must be an historical attack, one in which the United States would be devastated and it would place fear in the minds and hearts of governments and individuals from around the world. But also in order for the attack to be effective and for bin Laden to save face it must be on US home soil. September 11 fulfilled all of bin Laden's needs and then some, for the attacks became historical. They were (1) recorded as the deadliest terrorist act in world history; (2) the most devastating attack on US soil by a foreign entity since the Pearl Harbor attack by the Japanese in 1941; and (3) proved to be an indisputable and effective global recruiting tool for the radical Islamist. In 2003, bin Laden's sermon for the Feast of the Sacrifice (one of Islam's holy days in a year) was broadcast and recorded on the Al-Jazeera TV and the Al-Hayat, a daily London based newspaper, in which he not only quoted 9:5 from the Holy Qur'an but also before reciting the verse he praised and thanked Allah for revealing the *"verse of the sword"* to Muhammad in order to abolish falsehood and reveal the truth in the world. Bin Laden proved to the radical Islamic world that - *When Allah speaks, It is so!*

The second key area of Allah's commands is found in Surat 9:14.15 in which the twenty-first century Mujahid believe themselves to be not only the judges but also the executioners of Allah's divine wrath against all the nonbelievers: *"Fight them, and Allah will punish them by your hands, and disgrace them."* And for obeying Allah's commands they are promised that He will *"Help you (to victory) over them, heal the breast of believers. And still the indignation of their hearts."* Allah also in these verses redefines His supremacy by informing His loyal warriors that, *"Allah will turn (in mercy) to whom He will and Allah is an all-knowing. All wise."* It is these two revelations (commands) that have greatly influenced the profile of the present-day radical Mujahidin recruits who believe that Allah in his command identifies Himself as the sole cause of victory in their fighting. Surat 8:17 reaffirms these commands for the young recruits who believe: *"It is not ye who slew them; it was Allah. When thou threwest (a hand full of dust), it was not thy act, but Allah's; in order that He might confer on the believers a gracious benefit from Himself. For Allah is He who hearth and knoweth all things."* An excellent example of the power found within these two verses was how ISIS quoted them to justify their killings of Shiites, Kurds, and Christians in Iraq and Syria and in February of 2015 ISIS used part of verse 14 as the title of their video showing the brutal burning alive of the Jordanian pilot Muaz al-Kassasbeh: *"heal the breast of believers."*

This command, as noted in verses 14 and 15, is continued in verse 16, the third key command in Surat 9, in which Allah promises mercies unlimited only for those who *"strive with might and main"* and He questions them: *"Do you think that you would be left alone while Allah has not yet known? Those among you who strive with might and main, and take none for friends and protectors Except Allah, His messenger, and the (community) of believers? And Allah is well-acquainted with (all) that ye do."* For the radical Islamists Allah, in these three verses, has divided the world into *Da-al-Islam* (house of Islam) or *Dar-al-Harb* (house of war). Al-Qaeda and ISIS have proven any place in the world that is not submitting to Shari'ah law (Islamic Law) is in the House of War (*Dar-al-Harb*) which includes over half of the world including the United States. It is also this one principal that the global Jihadist movements have applied literally to brand governments and/or individual Muslims and non-Muslims, not only in the Middle East, from around the world as *Kufr*—non-believers—and therefore in the House of war or *Dar-al-Harb*. Sayyid Qutb, known as the Father of Jihad, reintegrated this command in the following statement found in his book *Milestones*: *"In the world there is only one party of Allah; all others are parties of Satan and rebellion. 'Those who believe fight in the cause of Allah, and those who disbelieve fight in the cause of evil. Then fight the allies of Satan; indeed, Satan's strategy is weak.' (4:76)* "Only one place on earth can be called the home of Islam (*Dar-al-Islam*), and that is the place where the Islamic state is established and the Shari'ah is enforced and Allah's limits are observed and where all the Muslims administer the affairs of the community with mutual consultation. The rest of the world is the home of hostility (*Dar-al-Harb*). A Muslim can have only two possible relations with *Dar-al-Harb*: peace with a contractual agreement, or war. A country with which Muslims may have a treaty is not regarded as the home of Islam" **(13).** An excellent example of a government being judged as being in the House of war or not being *only one party of Allah* is the nation of Egypt. During the Arab Spring Revolution, Mohamed Morsi, of the Muslim Brotherhood terrorist organization, was elected president of Egypt. Morsi won his election on promises to the citizens of Egypt of economic, social, political, and religious freedoms. However, upon the onset of his tenure as President of Egypt he enforced strict Shari'ah law and placed members of the Muslim Brotherhood terrorist organization in key political and military positions. After just a few months he was forced out of his position as president by a military coup. It was the force of Morsi from his post as president of Egypt that proved to be a perfect example for ISIS and other radical Islamist movements that a peaceful change from the House of War (*Dar al-Harb*) to the House of Islam (*Dar al-Islam*) is impossible. It is important here to understand that a Muslim is not defined by his nationality but rather by his faith and anywhere on earth that is ruled under Shari'ah law is automatically in the House of Islam. If you believe in Allah's revelations, as found within the Sacred Qur'an, then you are obligated to practice Islam as the Prophet Muhammad did and become a true **warrior of God**. For thousands of individuals throughout the world, and the fourth key command, Islam is the only **"religion of truth"** and therefore it is the only religion given for all mankind. Islam in Arabic means *"submission – submission only to the will of Allah."* For the twenty-first century Mujahid recruits they have answered Allah's call and have become His sacred army selected and commanded by Allah to rid the world of all evil. Their belief and that of all Muslims is founded in 9:29, in which Allah commands them that they are either to enslave all the nonbelievers or kill them: ***"Fight those who believe not in the last day, nor hold that forbidden which hath been forbidden by Allah and His messenger (Muhammad) nor acknowledge the religion of Truth, from among the People of the Book, until Jizya with willing they pay the submission and feel themselves subdued" (9:29).*** It is their interpretation of this verse that is paramount in comprehending who they see themselves as and why the world is divided into good and evil. For them Allah has not only defined His supremacy by commanding Islam as the only ***"religion of truth,"*** but He also has set no geographical boundaries as to where they were to enslave or kill all the nonbelievers and He commanded the eminence of Muhammad as their role model and His only messenger: ***"hold that forbidden which hath been forbidden by Allah and His messenger (Muhammad)."*** There is one more very important factor found within verse 29 and that is that Allah commands the dominance of Islam over all Jews and Christians—"*the People of the Book".* Like verse 5, the ***verse of the sword***, verse 29 abrogates all previous revelations referring to peace, mercy, compassion, kindness, and immunity for ***"the People of the Book" (14).*** Al-Qaeda, ISIS, and the radical Islamist movements have quoted verse 29 to justify their deliberate destructions to erase any evidence of sacred religious and/or archeological sites as idolatrous. For example, the destruction and bombing of the historical sixth century statues of the Bamiyan Buddha's in 2001 in Afghanistan by al-Quade/Taliban; the bombing of the sacred Imam Ali Mosque in Najif, Iraq, which contained the tombs of Ali, Adam, and Noah by al-Qaeda of Iraq (AQI) in 2003; the bombing of the tomb of the Biblical prophet Jonah (or Yunus) in Iraq by ISIS in 2014, in which they also destroyed the historical mosque that stood over the top of the tomb; or the destruction of the Temple of Baalshamin, a 2,000 year old UNESCO Heritage site in 2015 by ISIS; the destruction of the 3,000 year old archaeological site of Iraq's ancient Assyrian city of Nimrud in 2015; and recently the bombings in Yemen of two sacred Mosque frequented by Shiites. This is only a few of the many archeological and/or historical sites that they have destroyed in the twenty-first century. The pure nature of this new breed of Mujahidin is defined in verse 29, in which Allah makes it very clear that there can only be total submission, for it is **either/or** and nothing in between. Muhammad, peace be upon him, said: "I have been ordered to fight the people till they say: 'None has the right to be worshipped but Allah.' And if they say so, pray like our prayers, face our Qibla, and slaughter as we slaughter, then their blood and property will be sacred to us and we will not interfere with them except legally and their reckoning will be with Allah" **(15).**

Allah, in verses 9:38, 39, His fifth key command, makes an ultimatum for all Muslims by reprimanding them into making a choice between fighting gloriously and courageously with Him in His cause or remaining behind and clinging to some worldly gain and earthly need and being marked as a coward: *"O ye who believed! What is the matter with you, this when ye are asked to go forth in the Cause of Allah, ye cling heavily to the earth? But little is the comfort of this life, as compared with the Hereafter"* (9:38). *"Unless ye go forth, He will punish you with a grievous penalty, and put others in your place; but Him ye would not harm in the least, for Allah hath power over all things"* (9:39). In these two verses Allah rebukes their behavior for being hesitant in making the ultimate choice to join Him in His war against all evil and He has made it very clear that those who refuse to join Him in His cause He will punish *"with a grievous penalty"* not only in this life but also in their hereafter life. Muhammad, peace be upon him, said: "I heard Allah's Apostle saying, 'The example of a Mujahid in Allah's Cause—and Allah knows better who really strives in His Cause—is like a person who fasts and prays continuously.' Allah guarantees that He will admit the Mujahid in His Cause into Paradise if he is killed, otherwise He will return him to his home safely with rewards and war booty" **(16).** Allah promised humiliation and shame as part of His punishment for anyone refusing to join Him in His Cause of War not only **"with grievous penalty"** but also by *"putting others in your place."* This is a powerful ultimatum in a culture and society where *"shame"* and *"losing face"* is such a dishonorable and life-threatening alternative, not only for the individual but also for their family, their extended family, their tribe, and for the universal Muslim ummah. It is because of the power found in humiliation and shame for Arab/Islamic men that verses 9:29, 38, and 39 have become effective recruiting tools for the young potential mujahidin from around the world. Muslims fear Allah, for He is all sovereign and only He can send them to Paradise (Heaven). Therefore, since 1979 al-Qaeda, ISIS, and other radical Islamists have been following these four verses in their documented punishment of both Muslim and non-Muslims. During my studies and work within the Islamic regions I became enlightened by the knowledge that there are actually three types of Jihad obligations for all Muslims: (1) Jihad against one's true inner self, one's soul, known as *Jihad al-nafs;* (2) Jihad against demonic creatures led by Satan and known as *Jihad al-Shaytaan* (both *Jihad al-nafs* and *Jihad al-Shaytaan* are obligatory to everyone who is accountable to Allah); and (3) Jihad against hypocrites, the *Kufr* nonbelievers known as *Jihad munaafiqun,* in which all Muslims are obligated to fight. Plus I learned during my opportunities to sit and listen to the elders that Muhammad, peace be upon him, gave another obligation to his followers: "There is no Hijra (i.e. migration) from Mecca to Medina after the conquest (of Mecca), but Jihad and good intention remain; and if you are called by the Muslim ruler for fighting, go forth immediately" **(17).** When I sought clarification in reference to the meaning of this Sunnah (a portion of Muslim law based on Muhammad's sayings), "and if you are called (by the Muslim ruler) for fighting, go forth immediately" I learned that one is also obligated to follow the commands of a chosen leader, a man of great religious knowledge and a devout Muslim, for they are considered to be chosen by Allah and therefore have the highest authority on both the Qur'an and the Hadith. It is because of this command by Muhammad that young Mujahidin from around the world have become motivated and influenced by such role models and Islamic leaders as Suleiman the Magnificent, Ibn Taymiyah (who had an enormous influence on today's Jihadist mindset), Abul Ala Maududi, Sayyid Qutb, Abdullah Azzam (known as the father of Jihad), Ayatollah Ruhollah Khomeini, Sheikh Usama bin Laden, Abu Bakr al-Baghdadi (the newly self-appointed Caliph of ISIS), and various radical religious scholars, leaders, and Imams. One of the most powerful individuals who has had and still does have such an influence in the twenty-first century radical Islamist motivation and the enlisting of young martyrs is Sheik Omar Abdel-Rahman, also known as *"the blind Sheik"* from Brooklyn, N.Y., who stressed that now was the time and this is the generation and that all Muslims were obligated to join in Allah's cause to restore the soul of Islam and to purify the Muslim ummah by global Jihad (universal war). Sheik Abdel-Rahman was convicted of being the mastermind behind the 1993 World Trade Center terrorist bombing in New York City. For all devout Muslims throughout the world Allah's commands found in verse 9:29, 38 and 39 and the quoted sayings of Muhammad are each demands that they are obligated to respond to and perform. They are the **"chosen generation"** and Jihad is **"Fard'Ayn,"** an unconditional obligation, for they are compelled to serve Allah and to do whatever it takes to fulfill all of His commands throughout the world.

Allah's sixth key command found in Surat 9 elevates one's highest obligation as a Mujahid (*warrior of God)*, to that of martyrdom or *"shahid." "Shahid"* is an act of killing infidels in the battle for Allah and therefore it is not only **encouraged** but also **rewarded.** To receive this promised eternal reward one must make the ultimate of sacrifices, their life, and do it in the name of Allah only —**"Allah-u-Akbar."** — **"Allah-u-Akbar,"** which signifies that God is the creator and ruler of the universe and everything on and in it. The media has made a mockery of martyrdom by labeling these young warriors as *"suicide bombers "*instead of *"shahid"* or *"Martyrs for Allah."* In the Islamic faith, suicide, like in the Christian faith, is forbidden and recognized as a major sin. Suicide is the killing of oneself out of some form of personal despair or worldly problems and acting against the will of God. Unlike the martyr, a person who commits suicide has disconnected themselves from Allah, the one and only God—*Allah Akbar*— and therefore will receive His strictest of punishments. Both the Qur'an and the Sunnah/Hadith make it very clear that the most threatening mistake any individual can make, especially as a Muslim, is to separate themselves from the will of Allah (God). In Surat 4:29 and 30 Allah makes it very clear that suicide is forbidden: ***"O ye who believe! (Do not) kill yourself, for truly Allah has been to you Most Merciful. If any do that in rancor and justice, soon shall we cast him into the Fire?"*** The Prophet Muhammad, peace be upon him, made at least thirteen responses to the question of suicide within the Sunnah/Hadith. In the chapter titled Funerals (Al-Janaa'iz), Muhammad makes the following comments in reference to the severity and dishonor found in one who chooses to commit suicide: "He who commits suicide by throttling shall keep on throttling himself in the Hellfire (forever) and he who commits suicide by stabbing himself shall keep on stabbing himself in the Hellfire" **(18).** And "And if somebody commits suicide with anything in this world, he will be tortured with that very thing on the Day of Resurrection;" **(19)** and in Hadith 177, book 23 Muhammad makes the fearful command: "I forbid Paradise for him the person who commits suicide." Unlike the individual who commits suicide, a young Mujahid, who dies fighting for Allah's cause, is promised to become not only a witness for Allah but also His role model. Allah's command to become a *Shahid* is so paramount for all Mujahid that in verses 20, 38, 39, 52, 73, 88, and 111 in Surat 9 He makes very clear both the honor with which He will reward those who chose to make the ultimate sacrifice (He ***"has got ready Gardens (Paradise) under which rivers flow, to dwell therein forever. That is the supreme success"***) and the degree of dishonor and punishment He will inflict on those who fail to respond to His call (***"If not you go forth, He will punish you (with) a painful punishment, and will replace you (with) a people other than you, and not you can harm Him (in) anything. And Allah (is) on everything All-Powerful"*** (9:39).) This either/or promise is reinforced by

Muhammad, who promises the young Mujahidin (peace be upon him) that: "When anyone of you dies, he is shown his place both in the morning and in the evening. If he is one of the people of Paradise; he is shown his place in it, and if he is from the people of the Hell-Fire; he is shown his place therein. Then it is said to him, 'This is your place till Allah resurrects you on the Day of Resurrection' "**(20).** Because of the degree of fear that death and their afterlife holds in their daily lives this promise from both Allah and Muhammad has become a number one recruiting tool used most ardently by the radical Islamist leaders and Imams. Muslims, like Christians, believe that God weighs their good deeds and their bad deeds and then He and only He determines if they will go to heaven or hell. For upon a Muslim's death they will reside in either paradise (heaven) or hellfire until their day of resurrection. It is very clearly defined in the Qur'an, the Hadith, and Shari'ah law that for anyone who commits suicide and/or treason (the denouncing of their Islamic faith) the penalty is death and life in hellfire for eternity. In Surat 9:111, known as a *"Salvific* (leading to salvation) *covenant"* is a covenant made between God and man for, it is in this verse that Allah promises divine redemption for those who chose to make the ultimate of self-sacrifices: ***"Allah hath purchased of the believers their persons and their goods; for theirs (in return) is the Garden (of Paradise); they fight in His Cause, and slay and are slain: a promise binding on Him in truth, through the Torah, the Gospel, and the Qur'an: and who is more faithful to his Covenant than Allah? Then rejoice in the bargain which ye have concluded: that is the achievement supreme."*** This command is also found in Surat 2:154, in which Allah informs His followers: ***"And say not of those who are slain in God's cause. They are dead, nay they are alive but you perceive it not."*** He declares that ***"those who are slain in Allah's way are*** *not dead but alive"* (3:169). The key word for the radical Islamist is *"purchased"* and therefore the only way to actually prove their obedience to Allah is to make the ultimate sacrifice—*"slay or be slain,"* fighting in His declared war. Death in the way of Allah is a distinction which is honorable and desirable to these young mujahid, for they will never become distinct or perish for they will become *Shahid.* Their firm belief that Allah has purchased their soul, their fate, and their destiny **al-qadar** (the divine will and decree of Allah) is a powerful motivation for all Muslims. Surat *81:29: "And you do not will except that Allah wills—Lord of the worlds"* and Surat 3:143 and 145, *"that they had wished for martyrdom before you encountered it"* and that their death is planned and controlled by Allah only, *"And it is not [possible] for one to die except by permission of Allah at a decree determined"* exemplifies their belief in the divine will of Allah—*al-qadar. Al-qadar* is one of the five pillars in the Islamic faith. Muhammad Atta, the pilot of the first plane to crash into the World Trade Center on 9/11, quoted verse 143 in his farewell martyr letter to his family. Muhammad Atta and other young Mujahid did not commit this act of violence out of desperation, or genetic imbalance, or even to commit suicide, but rather they were acting on the belief of their faith and their obedience to the will of Allah who has purchased their souls. Sheikh Abdullah Azzam, in his biography *The Lofty Mountain,* stated that: "Islamic history is not written except with the blood of the martyrs" **(21).** To reject Allah's commands would reveal them not only to be cowards (infidels) in the eyes of other believers but worse is the fact that Allah has *purchased their soul* and the fear that their souls would perish by their denial would be catastrophic to any devout Muslim. These young mujahidin are compelled to offer their lives for Allah's service because by doing so they will be reconciled to Allah and become His witnesses for generations to follow.

Because Islam is the only **"religion of truth,"** as noted previously in Allah's fourth key command in Surat 9, apostasy *(murtadd)* is a serious offense with the ultimate punishment: execution. As I was informed on numerous occasions, apostasy in Islam, the seventh key command found in Surat 9, is equal to treason in the United States—or should I say used to be as our government has become very negligent in trying American citizens who have joined forces with the radical Islamists and killed American citizens. One who apostatizes in Arabic is called *"man artadd'an dinihi,"* which means "One who turns his back on religion." In short, the punishment for an apostate is worse than a nonbeliever according to Islamic law. Perhaps I can establish the importance of apostasy in Islam by defining what legally constitutes a Muslim? According to Shari'ah law (Islamic law), any individual who is born into Islam (meaning their father was a Muslim) or one who chooses to become a Muslim (converts of their own will) is legally considered to be a Muslim. An apostate is any individual who chooses to abandon and/or renounce their Islamic faith to become a Christian, Jew, or a member of another religious denomination. Muhammad, peace be upon him, said, "If somebody (a Muslim) discards his religion, kill him" **(22).** Islam is not only a religion but it is also a political state and since there are no geographical boundaries designated in Islam nor is there a separation between church and state, apostasy is not only a critical degrading influence on the universal Muslim ummah but it is literally an act of treason against the global state of Islam. Therefore, the punishment for apostasy is not negotiable as the Holy Qur'an, the sacred sayings and deeds of Muhammad, and Shari'ah law all proclaim death—"**kill him.**" I have always questioned the legality of President Barack Hussein Obama the II's international media claim that he had denounced his Islamic faith in lieu of the strict nonnegotiable punishment (death) to anyone who does so, according to the three most sacred texts and rulings to be found in Islam (The Holy Qur'an, The Sunnah/ Hadith and the Shari'ah Law). I was informed during my studies, work, and travel within the Islamic world that not only was the penalty death for the apostasy but that no devout Muslim could associate with, have any form of dealings with, and most definitely not be seen in the company of any Muslim who had denounced his or her faith for fear of their own life. Yet numerous prominent Muslims, including Imams, have met with and had their photos taken with our president. The Islamic law is very strict in that no individual who has denounced their Islamic faith is allowed to enter into any mosque anywhere in the world. Allah promises all who choose apostasy, leave the Muslim faith, severe punishment in both their life here on earth and in the hereafter. In 9:66 Allah makes it very clear to **"Make ye no excuses; ye have rejected Faith after ye accepted it."** And Allah continues this message in 9:73 and 74: **"They swear by Allah that they said nothing evil, but indeed they uttered blasphemy, and they uttered it after accepting Islam."** For Islamists following the example set by Muhammad, the penalty for denouncing one's Islamic faith, even in the twenty-first century, is death. I remember being told the story by several devout Muslim elders of Muhammad's conquering of Mecca in 629 and how he had ordered his army not to kill or punish the residents of Mecca who did not draw arms against them. But he did give orders that several individuals who had abandoned Islam and committed apostasy were to be killed. One such individual who Muhammad had declared the death sentence for was Abdullah ibn Sa'd, who had been a close member in Muhammad's inner circle and was one of the individuals who recorded a written transcript of Allah's revelations but who had abandoned Islam and now lived in the city of Mecca. Muhammad, peace be upon him, said, "If somebody (a Muslim) discards his religion, kill him. I will not sit down unless you kill him (as it is) the verdict of Allah and His Apostle" **(23).** No one can doubt the severity of apostasy in Islam, for Allah makes it clear **"So He hath put as a consequences Hypocrisy into their hearts, (to last) till the day whereon they shall meet Him because they broke their Covenant with Allah, and because they lied (again and again)"** (9:77). All of the quotes cited in this paragraph were recorded during the latter part of Muhammad's life and therefore they abrogate any previous revelations. Two prominent Islamic scholars who are highly respected within the Islamic community have written excellent manuscripts and books on the topic of Apostasy. They are Mufradat-gharb-ul-Qur'an-lil Sheik-ar-Raghib and Abdul Ala Mawdudi. I have read both of these gentlemen's' materials and books and recommend them for anyone interested in approaching this topic deeper. For the radical Islamist, apostasy is also someone who has not professed their faith in Allah and/or someone who reveals their disbelief in the supremacy of Allah. Radical Islamists believe that Allah has given them the authority, according to the quoted verses from the Surat and the Sunnah noted, to act as both the judge and the executioner of anyone who is guilty of apostasy. Therefore, according to Allah's commands and Muhammad's, the punishment of death is not negotiable: "Whoever changed his Islamic religion, then kill him" **(24).** One must remember that Allah gave Muhammad the authority to speak for Him as His last prophet. **"But if they have treacherous designs against thee (O Messenger), they have already been in treason against Allah, and so hath He given** *you power over them"* (Surat 8:71). In order to fully examine and justify my comments in regards to Islam and apostasy I sought answers as found within the Holy Qur'an, the Sunnah/Hadith, and Shari'ah law, and text from prominent Islamic scholars and scholars of Islamic law. Careful examination was given to Muhammad's sayings and deeds on this subject, as he is the role model for the twenty-first century radical Islamist. The reason I felt the necessity to include apostasy as the seventh key command of Allah is because it plays an important role in our lives and how we view Islam. For it is not my interpretation of how individuals should be treated who commit apostasy that is important, but rather an understanding of how Muslim scholars, scholars of Shari'ah law, the present day Mujahid, leaders of the twenty-first century radical Islamic movement, and the new Caliphate interpret this important doctrine and those who have believed it through the centuries from the time of Muhammad.

No chapter on Jihad would be complete without discussing the severity of punishment that al-Qaeda, ISIS, and other radical Islamists have forced on individuals whom they have judged to be *Kufur*—an infidel and/or a nonbeliever. Allah's ninth key command to His Mujahid in Surat 9 was the *"aggressiveness and harshness to be shown to the nonbelievers"* (9:1-6, 14-16, 73-74 and 123). The videos and media postings of their carnage, beheadings, torture, and their love for violence has left an impact on humans throughout the world. The Centers for Disease Control and Prevention defined such interpersonal violence as "the intentional use of physical force or power, threatened or actual, against another person or against a group or community that results in or has a high likelihood of resulting in injury, death, psychological harm, maldevelopment, or deprivation" **(25)**. Al-Qaeda, ISIS, and other radical Islamist Mujahid have always justified their beliefs and their acts of carnage and brutality as performing the **Highest Good** for the global Muslim ummah. For example, Abu Bakr al-Baghdadi, the newly self-declared Caliph of ISIS who holds a doctorate in Islamic studies from the Islamic University in Baghdad and who is knowledgeable in the sacred text found within the Holy Qur'an and the Hadith, professes that all of his Mujahid are only carrying out Allah's will. Because of his status as Caliph, Abu Bakr al-Baghdadi holds Allah's appointed authority for many young recruits throughout the world who have a deep love of violence and revenge. For Allah commands all Mujahid *"that they must fight them until Islam reigns supreme"* (2:193). Al-Baghdadi, Usama bin Laden, and other radical Islamist leaders have quoted from the Qur'an and the Sunnah/Hadith as proof that all of their mass murders, beheadings, crucifixions, and cruel and inhumane acts are justified and commanded by Allah himself. **It is the Islam that they practice that the world needs to not only know but also adhere to in their counter/terrorism strategies!** In addition to the previously quoted revelations found within Surat 9 there are significant verses found in Surat's 8, 5, and 47 which the twenty-first century radical Islamist Mujahid believe in and obey, all of which were revealed to Muhammad in the later years of his life, and therefore abrogate all previous verses of peace and nonviolence. *"Remember the Lord inspired the angels (with the message) I am with you; give firmness to the Believers I will instill terror into the hearts of the unbelievers. Smite ye above their necks and smite all their finger-tips off them"* (8:12). It is this Quranic verse plus verses 8:13 & 14 that al-Qaeda and ISIS have used in their released videos of the beheadings of international journalists, innocent citizens, even children, and mass decapitations such as the twenty-one Egyptian Coptic Christian migrant workers in Libya *"because they contended against Allah and His Messenger. If any content against Allah and His messenger Allah is strict to punish. Thus (will it be said): Taste ye*

then of the (punishment) for those who reject is the chastisement of the fire" (8:13 &14). ISIS justified their horrific cyber video of the young Jordanian pilot, Moath Kassassbeh, being doused with gasoline and set afire as **"the chastisement of the fire."** ISIS and other radical Islamist Mujahid have interpreted this revelation as a command from Allah that all nonbelievers are merely firewood for Hell. Allah commanded His warriors that once they entered into His Jihad and **"when you meet the unbelievers [in battle], <u>strike at their necks; at length, when ye have thoroughly subdued</u> them, bind (the captives) firmly: therefore (is the time for) either generosity or ransom; until the war lays down its burdens. Thus (are you commanded): but if it had been Allah's will, He could certainly have exacted retribution from them (Himself), but (He lets you fight) in order to test you, some with others. But those who are slain in the way of Allah, He will never let their deeds be lost"** (47:4). The degree of brutality that Allah commands His Mujahid is clearly defined in this verse. There are two Sunnah incidents, recorded in the Hadith, of Muhammad's motivational influence on the present day Mujahid ordering the beheadings of their captors: **"**The Jews were made to come down, and Allah's Messenger imprisoned them. Then the Prophet went out into the marketplace of Medina, and he had trenches dug in it. He sent for the Jewish men and had them beheaded in those trenches. They were brought out to him in batches. They numbered 800 to 900 boys and men. The affair continued until the Messenger of Allah had finished with them all" **(26).** And the second recorded incident found in Sahih Bukhari in Volume 5, Book 59, Numbers 443-446 account of the Prophet Muhammad's twenty-five day besiege on the rich Jewish settlement Banu Quraiza and demanded the unconditional surrender of all men who were sentenced to death by decapitation and the women and girls were raped and sold into slavery. The stories, which I was told about Banu Quraiza, by both

Muslim elders and young, placed the number of male decapitations range from 300 to 800, depending who was telling the story. "Unconditionally surrender of all men who were sentenced to death and the women and young girls raped and sold into slavery and their property Looted." It is the role model of Muhammad that today's Mujahid are imitating. As with their mass executions, ISIS has used the media, videos, and propaganda publications to justify their persecutions, rape, and sex slave trading of the women and young girls, married and/or un-married, of the ethnic minority religious group Yazidi by citing the following verses from the Holy Qur'an. In verses 5 and 6 of Surat 23 and in verse 24 of Surat 4, Allah states that sexual intercourse with their female captives is permissible: ***"Who guard their modesty, except with those to them in the marriage bond, or (the captives) whom their right hands possess, for (in their case) they are free of blame"*** (23:5 & 6). ***"Whom your right hands possess"*** are suitable victims for rape for they are ***"your property"*** and **"there is no blame on you, and Allah is All-knowing All wise"** (4:24). What makes this cruel and illicit treatment permissible is that these young women and girls are nonbelievers (*Kufr*) and therefore are from the world of *Dar-al Harb* (evil) which makes them the legal property of their captors to do with as they wish. Another excellent example of the power found within the Qur'an and how today's Mujahid justify their carnage is found in the published photos and articles on the crucifixion of their young captives: "Al-Qaeda-backed Jihadists are hanging the bodies of executed enemies on crosses crucifixion-style in a town in Northern Syria, according to a Syrian opposition group. Alrquaoui said he witnessed the executions himself, and took photographs that have since been posted on the group's facebook page, and are now being circulated on the Internet" **(27).** The most disturbing thing about these twenty-first century Mujahid is their love of violence and how easy it is for them to dehumanize and degrade any one whom they judge to be a *Kufr* (nonbeliever). They see themselves as Allah's legal judge and executioners.

It is very important for the reader to understand that the twenty-first century radical Islamists have not **and are not creating a new Islamic Jihad but are merely using the exact same Quranic commands from Allah that Muhammad and the seventh century Jihadist were motivated by and submitted to.** Not only must they submit to Allah's commands, as his warriors, but they must also obey the examples and sayings of Muhammad, Allah's last prophet. Each radical Islamist sees himself as surrounded by infidels who are hostile to him and his message of faith. The Mujahid must fight to the bitter end. They must win or die! There is not a third option for them, for Allah commands all Mujahid *"that they must fight them until Islam reigns supreme"* (2:193).

From the above quoted Quranic revelations of Allah and the text taken from the sacred sayings and deeds of His Last chosen prophet Muhammad, plus my analysis of each quoted text I have endeavored to answer the following key questions as I set forth in the writing of this chapter: (1) Why have individuals from different nationalities and different nations heard the call to become warriors of Allah? (2) Why are they so willing and eager to sacrifice their lives for an ideology that is over a thousand years old? (3) Why do some Muslims consider it their responsibility to wage a global war against Jews, Christians, and Muslims and non-Muslims? (4) Why has the radical Islamist claimed that Jihad is a mandatory obligation of all Muslims? And (5) why have I referred to them as *'warriors of Allah—God'*?

Surat 9:1: *"Jihad is a communal obligation."*

NOTES:

1. *Declaration of Jihad against the Americans Occupying the Land of the Two Sacred Places*, Usama bin Laden, fatwa, 1996.

2. Imam Abu Dawood, Book 37: Kitab al-Malahim [Battles], Hadith Number 4278.

3. Michael Rank, 2012, The Quran – Chapter 5, *From Muhammad to Burj Khalifa, pg.24.*

4. Sahih-Bukhari, Hadith, Volume 9, Book 93, Number 476, Narrated by Ibn Umar http://www.sahih-bukhari.com/Pages/Bukhari_993.php. (Retrieved 5/25/2017)

5. Twenty five prophets are mentioned by name in the Quran – Adam, Idris (Enoch), Nuh (Noah), Hud (Heber), Salih (Methusaleh), Lut (Lot), Ibrahim (Abraham), Ismail (Ishmael), Ishaq (Isaac), Yaqub (Jacob), Yusuf (Joseph), Shu'aib (Jethro), Ayyub (Job), Dhulkifl (Ezekiel), Musa (Moses), Harun (Aaron), Dawud (David), Sulayman (Solomon), Ilias (Elias), Alyasa (Elisha), Yunus (Jonah), Zakariya (Zachariah), Yahya (John the Baptist), Isa (Jesus), Muhammad. *"Of some messengers We have already told you the story; of others We have not; - and to Moses God spoke direct."* (Quran 4:164)

6. Ibid. *Sahih Sahihari,* Vol.1, Book: 2, Number 25, translation by Dr. M. Muhsin Khan – Sunnah. Com/bukhari) Bukhari (full name **Abu Abdullah Muhammad bin Ismail bin Burkhari** was born in 194 A.H. and died in 256 A.H. His collection of

Hadith is considered second to none. He spent sixteen years compiling it, and ended up with 2,602 Hadith. His criteria for acceptance into the collection were amongst the most stringent of all the scholars of the Hadith. Sahih Bukhari is divided into nine volumes, each of which has several books and each book contains many of the individual sayings and/or deeds of Muhammad.

7. Ibid. *Sahih Bukhari, Volume 6,* and Book 60, Number 13 narrated by Al-Bara.

8. Jalālad-Dīn Muhammad Rūmi, Annotated and Explained by Dr. Ibrahim Gamard and Gamard,'*Rumi and Islam',* SkyLight Paths Publishing, 2004, p. 161.

9. Ibid. Jalāl ad-Dīn Muhammad Rūmi, p.181.

10. Ibid. Sahih Bukhari: Vol. 1, Book 2, Hadith #7, **Narrated by Ibn 'Umar.**

11. David Cook, *"Understanding Jihad,"* Chapter—*Qur'an and Conquest,* University of California Press, 2005, p.10.

12. A listing of a just a few of the Quranic verses abrogated by 9:5 *"verse of the Sword"* are: 2:83,139,190, 191, 192, 217,256; 3:20, 28, 4:63, 80, 81, 84, 90, 91, 140, 5:2, 13, 99, 6:66, 68, 70, 90, 91, 104, 106, 107, 108, 112, 137, 159, 29:50.

13. Sayyid Qutb, '*Milestone Along the Road',* (*Ma'alim fi al-Tariq*), Chapter IX –A Muslims Nationality and Belief.

14. The Holy Qur'an, Surat 9 verse 29 also abrogates the following previous revelations: 2:109, 256 & 257, 3:111, 3:186, 5:13, 6:90, 91, 8:61, 29:46, 29:46, 60:89.

15. Ibid. Sahih al-Bukhari, Book of Prayers, Volume 1, Book 8, Hadith 44, Number 392, Narrated Anas bin Malik, https://sunnah.com/bukhari/8/44. (Retrieved March 12/2017).

16. Ibid. Sahih Bukhari, **Volume 4, Book 52, Number 46, Narrated by Anas bin Malik.**

17. Ibid. Sahih al-Bukhari, Book 56, Fighting *for the Cause of Allah (Jihad),* Chapter 1: *The Superiority of Jihad,* Hadith 2, Narrated by Ibn'Abbas,

18. Ibid. Sahih al-Bukhari, Book 23, Hadith 118, Number 1365, Narrated Abu Huraira.

19. Ibid. Sahih al-Bukhari, Book 78, Hadith 77, Number 6047, Narrated Thabit bin Ad-Dahhak.

20. Ibid Sahih al-Bukhari, book 23, Hadith 130, Number 1377, Narrated `Abdullah bin `Umar.

21. Shahed Dr. Sheikh Abdullah Azzam, *The Lofty Mountain, First Edition,* Azzam Publications, *BCM UHUD,* London, United Kingdom, *h t t p : / / w w w . a z z a m . c o m.* (Retrieved 4/3/2017)

22. Ibid. Sahih <u>Bukhari, Hadith Volume 4, Book 52 Number: 260,</u> **Narrated by Ikrima.**

23. Ibid. Sahih Bukhari, Hadith Volume 9, Book 89, Number 271, Narrated by Abu Musa.

24. Ibid. Sahih Bukhari, Hadith Volume 9, Book 84, Number 57, Narrated by 'Ikrima.

25. www.cdc.gov/violencepreventio. (Retrieved March 5, 2015)

26. Shahih Al-Tabari Hadith, Vol. 8, p. 35.

27. Robert Spencer, "Jihad Watch, Syria: Islamic jihadists apply Qur'anic punishment of crucifixion," April 30, 2014, 7:34am, http://www.jihadwatch.org/2014/04/syria-islamic-jihadists-apply-quranic-punishment-of-crucifixion. (Retrieved 5/10/2017)

V

THE TWENTY-FIRST CENTURY BATTLEFIELD: PSYCHOLOGICAL WARFARE

"In military operations, to attack the mind is superior; to attack fortifications inferior. Psychological warfare is superior, combat is inferior." Chu-Ko, circa 220 AD

"Those angry will be happy again. Those wrathful will be cheerful again. <u>But a destroyed nation cannot exist again; the dead cannot be brought back to life.</u>" SUN TZU, *"THE ART OF WAR*

"It is the nature of Islam to dominate, not to be dominated, to impose its law on all nations and to extend its power to the entire planet." Hassan al-Banna, known as the Father of Jihad and founder of the Muslim Brotherhood in his book *Milestones* (1)

Part of understanding and comprehending who the radical Islamists are is having a concise picture of **their battlefield**, a battlefield in which revenge and savagery is used to inflict fear and reveal the vulnerability of their targeted enemy and to invoke revolt and distrust within its enemies' citizens against its government. It is a battlefield based on *propaganda by deed.* Franklin Delano Roosevelt made a very astute and truthful statement when he stated: "In history, nothing happens by accident. If it happened, you can bet someone planned it." This is nowhere more evident than the present day nonconventional *"War on Infidels,"* a battlefield being executed by Allah's chosen warriors, called in war studies psychological warfare. So what is psychological warfare? It is strategically planned and orchestrated attacks on one's targeted enemy's strengths, weaknesses, vulnerabilities, beliefs, and emotions. WHO is their targeted enemy? America and all nonbelievers who live in the world of *Dar-al-Harb,* the world of war, rather they be Muslim or non-Muslim. There are two very important factors that the world of *Dar-al-Harb* needs to fully understand about this battlefield. The **first** major factor is that for the radical Islamist, their declared war against all infidels (evil) in the world is a war that cannot end until the entire world is declared *Dar-al-Islam.* In other words, and a strategic counterterrorism factor, this war will not end until the world of Islam has conquered all the world of evil and establish a universal Islamic ummah (community), or the world comes to an end. As numerous radical Islamist Mujahidin have claimed:*"we will either* win *or die."* The **second** major factor is that there are several different types of Jihad in an Islamic war commonly known as psychological warfare. Successful psychological warfare has proven to intimidate, demoralize, and influence the conscious and subconscious mind of their opponents. *Propaganda by deed* is a powerful and effective means incorporated into psychological warfare. Ibn Chaldean, a famous Muslim historian and philosopher, wrote the following in reference to the rewards and power found in Psychological Warfare:

> Throughout history many nations have suffered a physical defeat, but that has never marked the end of a nation. But when a nation has become the victim of a psychological defeat then that marks the end of a nation. **(2)**

The radical Islamist is carefully and strategically orchestrating and implementing propaganda by *"Jihad by the pen and media,"* deception *(makara)*, and lying and deception *(taqiyya)*, each of which have their roots in the Qur'an, the Sunnah/ Hadith, and Shari'ah law. It is not only the messages they use to increase the weaknesses and vulnerabilities of their chosen enemy but also how those messages are relayed and the effects they will have on the individual citizens and governments targeted that determine their psychological success. There is also the *"Jihad of Money,"* attacking and influencing the targeted enemies' international and national economy. And the classical Islamic solution to conflict resolution, *"Hudna,"* calm or peace, and in Islamic history it has come to mean a truce or to make temporary peace. After an in-depth research into all four of the Islamic schools of Jurisprudence I noted that all four schools specify that negotiated agreements and peace truces (Arabic Hudna—to make peace) have the following conclusions, which are also very evident and prominent in the present-day radical Islamist strategy for conflict resolution: (1) cannot exceed duration of a period of ten years based on Muhammad's example as found within the Sunnah; (2) can be repudiated if a situation arises that is more profitable and advantageous; and (3) intended purpose is to buy time to regroup and reorganize tactical strategies and/or forces. The four jurisprudence schools based their conclusions on Muhammad's, peace be upon him, treaty of Hudaibiya as recorded in the sacred Hadith. "By Allah, and Allah willing, if I take an oath and later find something else better than that then I do what is better and expiate my oath" **(3).** PLO Chairman Yasser Arafat is quoted as making the following statement when he returned to Tunisia after signing the historical *"**land for peace treaty**"* also known as *"**The Wye River Memorandum**"* with Israel Prime Minister Benjamin Netanyahu: "The Israelis are mistaken if they think we do not have an alternative to negotiations. By Allah I swear they are wrong. The Palestinian people are prepared to sacrifice the last boy and the last girl so that the Palestinian flag will be flown over the walls, the churches, and the mosques of Jerusalem." A major question I wish to inject here is: if the Islamist Jihadist is allowed to lie, feign loyalty, manipulate the media and the economy, to use deception and infiltration, and that all forms of truce are susceptible to further their efforts to win, then how legitimate are any executive agreements, treaties, truces, and/or negotiations they have agreed to?

As noted in previous chapters, the radical Islamists have proven both their capabilities and effectiveness in psychological warfare starting with the four major events during 1979 that changed the world's interest and outlook of the Middle East and the Islamic ummah. These events were: (1) the war between Afghanistan and the Soviet Union was the first call in centuries and the first ever global call for Muslims to defend a brother Muslim nation against non-Muslims, infidels; (2) the taking of American citizens as hostages at the start of the Iranian Revolution was an uprising, seizure, and war between the world of *Dar-al-Islam* and the world of *Dar-al-Harb*—good versus evil. Newt Gingrich stated, in reference to the Iran capture and takeover of the American Embassy and its personnel in 1979, in a Wall Street Journal article: "President Jimmy Carter, in his State of the Union address two months later, declared the American captives 'innocent victims of terrorism'" **(4);** (3) the attack and seizure of the Grand Mosque in Mecca by a group of radical Islamists who demanded that the Saudi Arabian government prove its legitimacy as a Muslim-ruled nation; and (4) the 1979 Camp David Agreement which led to the assassination of Egyptian President Anwar Sadat by members of his own military and members of the radical Islamist organization The Muslim Brotherhood. I must warn you that in reading this chapter one must understand and be willing to accept that by revealing the effective strategies, strengths, and infiltration implemented by the radical Islamist it will also reveal the weaknesses and vulnerabilities of which they and *their government are guilty.*

Before we proceed in discussing the radical Islamist use of deception, *makara,* which translates *"to plot"* or *"to scheme,"* it is vital to have an understanding and knowledge of what and who commands them to use this weapon. In Islam there are a number of circumstances when lying to nonbelievers, especially in war, is permissible and even COMPELLED and justified in the sacred text of the Qur'an, the Hadith, and Shari'ah law. In Surat 16:106 of the Qur'an, believers are told that "**there are circumstances that can compel a Muslim to tell a lie.**" These circumstances are:(1) to advance the cause and spread of Islam; (2) in gaining the trust of a kufur - nonbeliever; (3) in time of war to reveal and use the targeted enemies vulnerabilities and weaknesses; (4) lying when the end justifies the means, *Kitman,* lying by omission; and (5) when one's honor is at stake—lying to save face, *lihifz ma´ alwajh* "to save face. Muhammad, peace be upon him, stated *"War is deceit"* **(5).** Eric Hoffer, an American moral and social philosopher and one of my favorite philosopher authors, wrote: "Propaganda does not deceive people; it merely helps them to deceive themselves" **(6).** This one quote is a perfect description as to WHY the radical Islamist has chosen a psychological battlefield. I believe there are three major strategies in which the radical Islamists have chosen and are implementing to influence and control their targeted enemies' mind-set and decision-making: number **one** is **FEAR** by savagery, threats of savagery, and the use of the media; number **two** is **INFILTRATION** by gaining access into the targeted enemies' infrastructure by using deception, "interfaith dialogue," propaganda, and the use of the media; and number **three** is their twenty-first century interpretation of the **HEGIRA** or also known as **Hijrah** (the legacy of the Prophet Muhammad, peace be upon him, translates to migration, a wave into one's targeted enemies' country by deception, propaganda, and the use of the media). Each of these three prime implemented strategies work well together and/or individually, as is evident in the following descriptions and detailed documented examples.

Their brazen publicized acts of the beheading of their captured victims have traumatized the world. In the mind of the radical Islamists these shocking acts inflict a lasting **fear** into the hearts and minds of the targeted enemy. But in reality they are actually only the warnings and the preparation for the battles that will follow. These shocking acts are not performed at random nor are they acts of craziness but are carefully planned and part of their overall strategy to leave a lasting impression in the minds of their targeted enemies—**propaganda by deed**. There is a lesson to be learned in each and every published act of their carnage and brutality; however, many individuals have chosen to deny this lesson and ignore or even refuse to accept the identifiable proof that they have revealed their battlefield, one in which the world is divided between good (them) and evil (their targeted enemy). Abu Bakr Naji, author of *The Management of Savagery*, advocates, "that savagery is a stage that the Muslim Jihadist must pass through in establishing a true Islamic universal ummah (community)" **(7).** There have been many speculations as to Abu Bakr Naji's true nationality and the exact date of publication, but it has been quoted numerous times in various radical Islamist publications including the Muslim Brotherhood and it was posted in its entirety on the al-Qaeda internet magazine *Sawt al-Jihad* in 2004. Najis manuscript has become one of the most published and widely quoted works noted in the radical Islamist movement. Naji also specified "that if the Jihadist fails in establishing this universal ummah then they must increase their savagery until they have accomplished this find—all will of Allah—all mankind as true" **(8).** As hard as it has been for many Americans, including many of their elected government representatives, to comprehend and accept the reasoning behind all of their brutal and in-humane acts of violence and carnage, I can assure you that each reported incident has been strategically and carefully instigated for their chosen audience.

In order for the radical Islamist to attract and maintain the publicity necessary to generate this widespread fear they must engage in increasingly dramatic, violent, and high-profile savagery. WHY? Because their high-profile savagery and fear tactics have provided and assured them nine positive and very effective psychological results: **First,** the more horrific and dramatic the act, such as the beheading of the twenty-one Egyptian Christian workers in Libya, the more publicity coverage the media gives them, which in turn insures the more widespread their fear factor is generated. In this dramatically staged violent act, the row of twenty-one Egyptian victims, each wearing bright orange jumpsuits, hands tied behind their backs and forced onto their knees in front of twenty-one radical Islamic judges and jurors who were covered from head to toe in black created a lasting image of superiority and imposed fear. In this staged and dramatic image the mujahidin presented a positive and lasting image of just who is from the *Dar-al-Harb* (the world of war—the world of evil) attired in bright orange kneeling before the righteous from the *Dar-al-Islam* (the world of Islam— Allah's chosen warriors) attired in total black. Another chilling and blatant dramatic orchestrated example of who is from the world of Islam and who is from the world of evil is the burning alive of the young Jordanian pilot locked in a cage while the warriors of Allah, once again attired from head to toe in black from the world of *Dar-al-Islam*, stand by watching and cheering as they, the judge and jury, observe their victim scream and be burned alive. These two highly global published incidents were staged and dramatized as examples to not only incite fear and terror but also to plant in the mind of their targeted enemy what to expect in the future. In Surat 8:12: ***"I [Allah] am with you, so strengthen those who have believed. I will cast terror into the hearts of those who disbelieved so strike [them] upon the necks and strike from them every fingertip."*** **Second,** the radical Islamist believes their violent acts of savagery are actually showing mercy to their victims because their killing of infidels and apostates is more merciful than what Allah would do to them on the *Day of Judgment*. Allah demands that all infidels and all apostates be made to pay the ultimate price with no leniencies for they have brought shame and dishonor to Allah and to the universal Islamic ummah (community). *"If anyone desires a religion other than Islam (submission to God), never will it be accepted of him; and in the Hereafter he will be in the ranks of those who have lost (All spiritual good"* (3:85). *"Kill all non-believers where you may find them"* (9:5), and a conscious abandonment and/or converting from Islam *"apostasy in Islam is worse than being an infidel"* (9:66, 73, 74 and 77). **Third,** their acts of savagery have provided a special bond of comradeship and self-esteem for the mujahidin, for through each dramatized carnage incident they are communicating their message that the world is divided into only two entities—good versus evil— and that they are Allah's chosen warriors, therefore they are from the world of good. It is because of this one factor that as Allah's warriors they have received the right to act as His judge, jury, and executioner. It is not surprising that in fulfilling Allah's call and will for a *Dar-al-Islam* (world of Islam/world of good) that the twenty-first century Jihadist takes great pride in their savagery. This pride is also founded in their belief that each act of savagery is paying tribute to the statesmanship and warrior leadership of the Prophet Muhammad. One must always remember that Islam from 632 to 1920 was not only a religious faith but it was also a political power that was ruled by military force and its strong ideology. History has proven how cults and/ or cult like movements that are highly motivated and led by a charismatic leader will have a strong brotherhood and cult like bond that will justify and unify committing acts of violence— such acts as the genocide documented in Rwanda, Sudan, Russia, the Nazi party, the crusades, the Mongolian invasions, and the early Islamic expansion just to name a few. For the twenty-first century radical Islamist their guiding principle is found in the Quranic verse 4:74:

> *So let those who fight in the cause of Allah who
> sell the life of this world for the Hereafter. And
> he who fights in the cause of Allah and is killed
> or achieves victory - We will bestow upon him a
> great reward.*

This one Quranic verse has created a special bond of comradeship, self-esteem, and pride in each dramatized carnage incident **and therefore** made each young Jihadist believe he is a live weapon for Allah. A **fourth** positive and proven effective strategy is the more violent their threat is and the more brutal and in-humane the actual act of violence is the more attention they receive and the more extensive the global media coverage they are guaranteed. The 9/11 attacks became the first and the beginning of a true live *reality TV show*, as individuals from around the world watched this catastrophic event unfold from the impact of the second airplane, the explosion, the collapsing of both World Trade Center towers, and the trauma inflicted on its victims. Usama bin Laden noted after the event that it was more influential and more catastrophic to America and the world then he and al-Qaeda had anticipated and it became a number one recruiting tool around the world, thanks to the extent and length of time that the media gave to them and to the event. Sad as it may seem, some of our present-day media searches for, invents, and yes, even sometimes causes some of the recorded and documented carnage that our nation and the world has been forced to witness. The recognized phrase for this event, *9/11*, was actually coined by the media, not by the actual terrorists who referred to it as *"Holy Tuesday."* The twenty-first century radical Islamists have fully mastered how to use the global social media to intimidate and support their fear propaganda and as an international recruiting tool. Abu al-Athir

Amr al-Absi, known in the international media sector as the *"Propagandist to God,"* is noted for his clever and accurate understanding of how to use the social media to not only promote their ideology and carnage but also to recruit for ISIS and the radical Islamist global movement. A **fifth** powerful and influential emotion and a strong mind-set found within the Arab and Islamic heritage is a *"loss of face"* that is rooted in shame and humiliation. This *"loss of face"* is inherited from one generation to the next and continues until a generation is born that can erase the humiliation and shame. The Islamic community believes that their forefathers had angered Allah and therefore all Muslims throughout the world were severally punished and caused to suffer great shame, humiliation, and loss of respect and honor throughout the world. This fall from social grace and a *loss* of dignity or *loss of face* must be revenged and removed in order for the universal Islamic ummah (community) to regain its status with Allah. Leaders, such as Hassan al-Banna, founder of the Muslim Brotherhood; Abdullah Yusuf Azam, known as the Father of Global Jihad; Ayatollah Ruhollah Khomeini, leader of the Iran Revolution; Usama bin Laden, founder of al-Qaeda, spiritual guide of Hezbollah Muhammed Hussein Fadlallah, and Abu Bakr al-Baghdadi, self-appointed Islamic Caliphate and head of ISIS, have molded their supporters into hostility and suspicion of all nonbelievers. Radical thinking Muslims throughout the world have been convinced that they are the generation chosen by Allah to rectify and remove all previous and present shame and humiliation. Plus, if one listens to the Islamic radical leader's rhetoric, it is also this twenty-first century generation that has been chosen, by Allah, to establish a universal united Islamic ummah under the Divine Rule of Allah—Shari'ah law. A universal community that is a copy of the original seventh century ummah as established by Muhammad in Medina. **Sixth,** their brutal dramatic and odious acts have proven to be a positive and a very successful global recruiting tool. As erroneous as it may seem, their acts of violence actually have a domino effect, for the more violent their acts are, the more media publicity they generate, which in turn generates confidence and patriotism, which generates an attachment to one's homeland and produces an attachment to the early generation of Islamic warriors. This domino effect of confidence and loyalty seems to be their strongest enthusiasm and pursuit rather than their actual Islamic faith. The need for confidence, loyalty, and an attachment to Muhammad and the early Islamic warriors has produced their violence in the name of their religious faith. The world for the radical Islamist is very simple and clear-cut for it is divided into only two compartments: the world of Islam (which is good) and the world of war (which is evil). With the world only consisting of two components, good and/or evil, and the only world of good is Islam, it is easy to understand why their extreme violence and savagery has been able to recruit so many young Muslims from around the world. In order for a territory and/or nation to be classified as *Dar-al-Islam*, its moral, social, and political laws must be ruled and controlled only by Shari'ah law. This is nowhere more exemplified than in the personified *homegrown terrorist syndrome,* which the global world is facing more and more in the twenty-first century. The *homegrown terrorist syndrome* are citizens of a state who plan and target their fellow citizens in an effort to instill fear and physical harm and to prove their commitment and loyalty to Islam and to prove that they are from the world of good. An excellent example of how effective their propaganda and savagery has been in recruiting young Muslims from around the world in creating the *homegrown terrorist syndrome* would be the Boston Marathon bombers. Two brothers of dual citizenship, Dzhokhar Tsarnaev, American/ Kyrgyzstan citizenship, and Tamerlan Tsarnaev, American/ Russian citizenship, plotted and instrumented what the media has penned as the *"pressure cooker bombings"* that killed three and wounded at least 265 individuals on April 15 of 2013. What makes this bombing more intriguing is that in the 2010 Summer edition of the al-Qaeda's magazine **Inspire,** an article was published in English titled *"How to make a bomb in the kitchen of* your mom," which described how to use everyday materials to make a "pressure-cooker bomb." The published article and the pressure-cooker bombs used in the Boston bombing were identical. This twenty-first century syndrome of violence in the name of Islam is not unique to the United States, for on July 7, 2005, in London four young British-born citizens chose to become part of the twenty-first century Quranic Revolution when they detonated consecutive bombs in the London underground and a local transit bus, killing fifty-six including the four (suicide) Islamic martyrs and injuring at least 784 fellow citizens. The London bombing by homegrown terrorist syndrome was *penned* by the media as the *"7/7 bombings."* The previous are only two examples of just how effective, worldwide, the savagery and grandiose carnage has served as a recruiting tool for the radical Islamists and also proven for so many individuals that the world is only made up of two components—good versus evil. It is not difficult to note by all of the global propaganda and media coverage given to each *homegrown terrorist syndrome* incident that the domino effect I spoke of earlier is so effective and has proven to be such a positive strategy for the radical Islamist in their psychological warfare. Adolf Hitler's Minister of Propaganda and National Enlightenment Joseph Goebbels was quoted as saying: "The essence of propaganda consists in winning people over to an idea so sincerely, so vitally, that in the end they succumb to it utterly and can never escape from it." The **seventh** proven strategy is the fear factor and how easy and effective it is to influence the political decisions in a democratic nation. Justice and laws in a democratic society are established by man, and therefore, can be altered and eliminated by man; however, in an Islamic society justice and laws are established by the sovereign will of Allah and therefore cannot be changed or ratified. History has proven a democratic society has powerful influences, either positive or negative, on its government's decisions and laws and is the easiest and most effective society to infiltrate. The **eighth** important factor is that these acts of violence between the Sunni and the Shiites are reigniting the old revenge flames that have existed in the history of Islam and that have caused numerous blood baths since the death of Muhammad in 632 AD. Islamic history has recorded how these two major denominations of Islam will fight side by side to destroy a common enemy but then turn on each other to determine who will be the ruling Muslim order. The old Arab proverb *"the enemy of my enemy is my enemy to rid our common enemy but they are still my enemy"* is still very prominent and alive even between Muslims. A **ninth** positive factor in the mind of the radical Islamist, and the most frightening, is that in order to attract and maintain their fear status in the hearts and minds of their targeted audiences and to continue their high-profile international publicity they must engage in even more dramatic, violent, and legendary savagery. These shocking acts are not performed at random nor are they acts of craziness but are carefully planned and part of their obligated duty that has only two outcomes: ridding the world of all evil or destroying the world. Whichever happens is strictly in the control of Allah. I believe the reality is that all of their dramatized brutality and carnage is actually only the warnings and preparation for the battles which will follow. In other words, the radical Islamist is warning the world of their capabilities and their determination to carry out their obligated duty to rid the world of all infidels. Abu Bakr Naji, author of *The Management of Savagery*, advocates that savagery is a stage that the Muslim Jihadist must pass through in establishing a true Islamic universal ummah (community). Naji also states that if the Jihadist fails in establishing this universal ummah than they must increase their savagery until they have accomplished this final will of Allah **(9)**—**a** world ruled only by Allah's justice under Shari'ah law!

Propaganda by deed would best describe the present-day brutality of the global Jihad movement. Their techniques have not only revealed their bravery to their fellow comrade jihadists but they have also revealed their dedicated obligation toward Allah's call for justice and a world ruled by Shari'ah law. The radical Islamist has perfected persuasive propaganda to an art, not only by publicizing their dramatic acts of savagery but also by methodically mastering the release of such acts of violence to achieve their intended response from their intended targets. The savage filmed beheadings of American hostages Daniel Pearl, Nick Berg, Peter Kassig, James Foley, and Steven Sotloff were staged symbolic expressions to inflict shock and fear into the hearts and minds of the American citizens. The brutally filmed death of the young Jordanian Muslim pilot was staged to send humiliation and a strong message to the Muslim nations who support America and its allies. This one staged brutality also sent two very powerful and strong messages to the international community: (1) that Muslims are not exempt from their judgment and justices and (2) that their level of savagery has and will continue to increase. Each of these are examples that exemplify why I refer to their staged and filmed press releases as *"propaganda by deed"* for they are not only a means to inflict shock and fear but also are a powerful and positive means to send a very deliberate message. That message is that this new breed of Islamist mujahidin's are grounded in their religious beliefs and commitments to carry out Allah's will and as His chosen warriors they have the right to decide who will live and who will die. To add credibility to their savagery they quote from the three most sacred texts in Islam: the Qur'an, the Sunnah/ Hadith, and the Divine Law of Allah—Shari'ah law—and from various historically recognized Islamic scholars and stories told of the religious traditions and bravery of the early Muslim fighters. They have modeled their brutality and propaganda strategies after the Prophet Muhammad and the first Muslim caliph, Abu Bakr in the seventh century. A bit of trivia: The present self-proclaimed Caliph, Abu Bakr Baghdadi, selected his title name to be Abu Bakr after the first Caliph following Muhammad's death in 632 AD. Caliph Abu Bakr was a trusted friend of the Prophet, the Prophet's first convert, made the night journey with the Prophet and was the Prophet's father-in-law. Abu Bakr Baghdadi is the first Caliph for the Muslim ummah since the fall of the Ottoman Empire following WWI. There was no coincidence in Abu Bakr Baghdadis selection of his title name as the new Caliph. No one can deny the persuasive ***"propaganda by deed"*** techniques that the radical Islamists have deliberately used to manipulate and shape their targeted audience's emotions and reactions. You may question my train of thought and claim that it is impossible to manipulate a mass of individuals into the propagandist mind-set, but I remind you of Adolf Hitler and the Nazi party's ability to turn and control the opinions and actions of thousands of individuals through their cleverly and deliberately controlled use of the media, staged films, and radio broadcasting, and their propaganda implementation of their Nazi policies.

Fear can only be inflicted and effective when your enemy's faith is destroyed. When the citizens of a nation lose their faith and confidence in their government they first turn on the very ones who sacrifice their lives daily to protect and allow the freedoms that they enjoy, expect, and demand. The scary factor in this truth is that as the problems develop and escalate, then the more savage the citizens become toward the very people who have taken oaths to protect them. This is no were more evident than in the deliberate killings of five police officers in Dallas, Texas, on July 7, 2016, and the ambush killing of three police officers in Baton Rouge, Missouri, on July 17, 2016. The twenty-first century movement *Black Lives Matter* is another perfect example of how easy it is for the radical Islamists to use savagery and racist tactics of fear, infiltration, and media propaganda to enhance violence and divide the American society. According to the UN Declaration of Human Rights, *all lives matter* for one's human rights is not dictated by the color of one's skin or by one's gender. Eric Hoffer in his book *The True Believer: Thoughts on the Nature of Mass Movements* made the following accurate assessment: "A movement is pioneered by men of words, materialized by fanatics, and consolidated by men of action" **(10).** Chairman Mao-Tse-Tung, founding father of the People's Republic of China, made the following connection to justify how effective propaganda and infiltration of the targeted enemy's masses can destroy a nation's survival: "The revolutionary war is a war of the masses; only mobilizing the masses and relying on them can wage it" **(11).** "Be Concerned with the Well-Being of the Masses, Pay Attention to Methods of Work" **(12).** History has proven that a nation's society collapses according to the degree of corruption found in their religion, moral values, social iniquities, government values, and priorities. When a society collapses it causes a defined breakdown in the whole infrastructure of that nation, which allows your enemy to take control of the government, the military, the police, intelligence, the education, the judicial and economic structure, and the social structure. Is this where America, in 2018, has allowed itself to be driven and programmed by the radical Islamist? I am referring to the outbreak of riots, propaganda, and various statements made by elected officials during and following the 2016 presidential election and that have continued into new administration term. It is obvious by the result of the elections that the majority of Americans decided they wanted a complete change in their elected government representatives and its national security platform. No such citizen outbreaks and violence occurred because of the 2008 and/or the 2012 presidential elections. Why? I believe that Americans need to ask the following three questions honestly: First, **who** is the leader behind this violent outbreak of hatred and revenge? Riots and citizen outbreaks do not occur without a well-planned strategy and an instigator (leader) who incites the violence. Secondly, **who** stands to win the most from inciting, promoting, supporting, and controlling a collapse and division among the American citizens and its infrastructure? There is always someone behind citizen uprisings who stands to win even at the cost of their fellow citizen's lives and welfare. Thirdly, **who** is responsible for organizing and carefully manipulating and ***"mobilizing the masses and relying on them to wage it?"*** A well-trained propagandist always watches for the right timing and to take advantage of every critical social situation noted within the targeted enemy's infrastructure. The destruction of peace is always caused by the incitement of some undercurrent which usually prefers to remain hidden and out of public view that has a cause that is beneficial, to themselves and to take advantage of their public status to get what they want. Incitement is the term I use to refer to individuals and/or a group of individuals whose statements and actions encourage hatred and anger, which in turn provokes violence, which in turn supports or promotes terrorist activity. I personally believe that incitement is far more lethal than someone giving a "hate speech" as it not only has the power to delegitimize its intended target but it encourages and supports violence and does in fact promote terrorist attacks. Psychological warfare is capturing the minds of your enemy's citizens, which in turn allows you to capture and control their souls, their attitudes, their decisions, and their actions. In order for any propagandist to be affective in any country they must rely on and incorporate the media to get their message out to and to mobilize the masses! The Nazi party instigated the masses to riot in Germany against their government by incorporating and controlling the media to gain control and power prior to WWII. The acts of violence which have resulted in these recent **hate campaigns** within America have not only taken a toll on human lives but have deteriorated the very tenets on which the nation of America was founded. Just like the radical Islamic terrorists, the perpetrators have refused to have any type of peaceful negations. I ask you: does Chairman Mao-Tse-Tung's message describe the twenty-first century United States?

Despite the apparent absence of a direct link between the various radical Islamic terrorist incidents and the riots and the citizen unrest, there is a constant stream of incitements to violence and hatred against and within America, as noted in the Muslim

Brotherhood "Phased Plan," a doctrine that describes various strategies to gradually influence and neutralize the American infrastructure and to demand that Shari'ah replace Western law **(13)** and in their recognition of and their implementation of Sun Tzu's principles to gain power over and control their targeted enemy. Although written over 2,000 years ago in China, Sun Tzu is still the ultimate authority on the art of psychological warfare and is studied in every nation's war college.

> To **capture** the **enemy's** entire **army** is better than to **destroy** it; to take intact **a regiment, a company, or a squad** is better than to **destroy** them. For to **win one hundred victories in one hundred battles** is not the acme of **skill**. To subdue the **enemy without fighting** is the supreme excellence. Thus, what is of supreme importance in **war** is to **attack** the **enemy's** strategy. Next best is to **disrupt his alliances by diplomacy**. The next best is to **attack his army**. And the worst **policy** is to **attack cities. (14)**

Sun Tzu's philosophy is "To subdue the **enemy without fighting** is the supreme excellence. Thus, what is of supreme importance in **war** is to **attack** the **enemy's strategy**." History has proven that the use of Sun Tzu's strategy has rendered one's targeted adversary to complete confusion and vulnerability not only within their society but also within their government and their military. The second major strategy used by the radical Islamists is infiltration, which characteristics include incitement and infiltration within the targeted enemy's infrastructure. The radical Islamists are proven masters in the skill of infiltrating a *Dar-al-Harb* territory, non-Muslim territory, according to a study into the strategies for infiltration used by their role model Muhammad and his planned Hijrah, of his persecuted converts, to Ethiopia and Yathrib, Medina, from Mecca in the seventh century. Like Muhammad, their success is made possible by their implanting of individuals who have been trained and transformed into the beliefs, attitudes, and mind-set of their targeted enemy's social and political structure and who are committed to Islam. Their strategy is patience and to be readily acceptable and to infiltrate surreptitiously and gradually, especially in order to acquire secret information and to influence their targeted enemy's beliefs, attitudes, and actions. The American people and their government are so caught up on the number of various terrorist attacks and being politically correct that they have allowed the radical Islamic Jihadist to indulge in infiltration, a form of psychological manipulative warfare, into the nation's complete infrastructure. No area within the American infrastructure has not been targeted and threatened by some form of infiltration and manipulation by the twenty-first century radical Islamist Jihadist movement under the leadership of the International Muslim Brotherhood, *Ikhwan* terrorist organization. (Chapter I, **"Revival of the Radical Islamist: The Muslim Brotherhood"**, describes in detail their power and capabilities in the art of infiltration and relationship with the radical Islaimist.) A full description of the MB strategies, plans, and tools being used in accomplishing their infiltration and takeover and conversion of America to an Islamic state was recorded in a document titled *"An Explanatory Memorandum on the General Strategic Goal for the Group in North America"* which was found during a federal investigator's search of the residence of Ismael Elbarasse, founder of the Dar Al-Hijra mosque in Falls Church, Virginia, in 2004 and entered as evidence in the 2008 Holy Land Terror

Funding Trial **(15).** The purpose of this document, dated May 22, 1991 and approved by the Shura Council states:

> Enablement of Islam in North America, meaning: establishing an effective and stable Islamic Movement led by the Muslim Brotherhood which adopts Muslims' causes domestically and globally, and which works to expand the observant Muslim base, aims at unifying and directing Muslims' efforts, presents Islam as a civilization alternative, and supports the global Islamic state, wherever it is. **(16)**

The document continues by describing the International Muslim Brotherhoods infiltration as a *"Civilization-Jihadist Process"* or sabotaging America from *"within"*:

> The process of settlement is a **"Civilization-Jihadist Process"** with all the word means. The Ikhwan must understand that their work in America is a kind of grand Jihad in eliminating and destroying the Western civilization from within and "sabotaging" its miserable house by their hands and the hands of the believers so that it is eliminated and God's religion is made victorious over all other religions. Without this level of understanding, we are not up to this challenge and have not prepared ourselves for Jihad yet. It is a Muslim's destiny to perform Jihad and work wherever he is and wherever he lands until the final hour comes, and there is no escape from that destiny except for those who chose to slack. But,

would the slackers and the Mujahidin be equal.
(17)

The document continues to expand on each of the key areas in which the Muslim Brotherhood has strategic plans on how to sabotage America's infrastructure: (1) all educational aspects, an example of this is how "In 1962, the Muslim Students Union was founded by a group of the first Ikhwans (MB) in North America and the meetings of the Ikhwan became conferences and Students Union Camps" **(18)**; (2) both the Democratic and Republican political parties and all local and national government organizations; (3) daily and weekly media newspapers, magazines, radio, television, and all audio, visual, and production centers; (4) economic organizations, investment projects, Islamic endowments, and the establishment of an Islamic central bank; (5) scientifically by becoming active in professional organizations including research centers and all technical and vocational training centers; (6) cultural and intellectual centers for studies and research and cultural and intellectual societies and foundations; (7) social welfare and charities, social organizations; (8) central and local youth clubs and foundations; (9) institutes for security training; and (10) all intelligence and military branches. The above noted MB document was confiscated along with various other instrumental and strategic materials including *"A List of Our Organizations and Organizations of Our Friends,"* which identified twenty-nine groups that would serve as fronts, were confiscated in a federal investigation at the residence of Ismael Selim Elbarasse in Annandale, Virginia. Elbrasse and his wife were arrested in August 2004 after being caught videotaping the Maryland's Chesapeake Bay Bridge intricate structure from their SUV. The investigation proved that Elbarasse was a member of the Islamic

Association of Palestine and a Hamas financial supporter and activist. The investigation also discovered that Elbarasse was the assistant to and even shared a checking account with Mousa Abu Marzook, the political director of Hamas. Elbarasse is just one of probably thousands of well-placed operatives for the Muslim Brotherhood *"civilization Jihad in America."* The tracing of the accomplishments of Abdurrahman Alamoudi, also known as Abdul Rahman al-Almoudi, accomplishments as an infiltrator operative in America for the Muslim Brotherhood reveals how effective the radical Islamist movement *"civilization Jihad project in America"* is and just how vulnerable and naive Americans are. Alamoudi immigrated to America in 1979 but did not become a naturalized American citizen for seventeen years, in 1996, but was able to acquire an authorized top-security clearance that allowed him to establish an elaborate operative history that included three presidential administrations, the Pentagon, the media, and even into the nation's military. What is paramount in tracing Alamoudi's operative career is noticing just how vulnerable and easy it was to infiltrate within America's infrastructure! Before he became a naturalized citizen in 1996 he founded the Islamic Society of Boston and served from 1985 to 1990 as an executive assistant to the president of the SAAR Foundation, an organization founded by the Muslim Brotherhood and an umbrella for over one hundred charities (which are still active), various think tanks, and financial and business institutions operated from their headquarters in Virginia. In 1990 he founded the American Muslim Council, an active organization listed under the umbrella of the Muslim Brotherhood, and in 1991 he made a strategic move that placed him deeper into America's national security with the US Defense Department as founder and organizer of a very powerful organization that is still in existence today known as the

American Muslim Armed Forces and Veterans Affair Council (AMAFVAC). With this one move, Alamoudi, a non-nationalized citizen, had the authority in selecting, training, and endorsing Muslim chaplains in our Armed Forces and the American Veterans organizations. Among such chaplains was James Yee, who eventually would be arrested in 2003 on suspicion of espionage, and Major Nidal Malik Hasan, an Army psychiatrist, who in 2009 went on shooting rampage killing thirteen and injuring over thirty military personnel on the US Fort Hood Military Base in Texas. The chaplains who were approved were mostly graduates from the Graduate School of Islamic and Social Sciences, the first privately independent institution established for the sole purpose of teaching Islamic studies in America, and run by Almoudi's close friend Taha Jabir Al-Alwan. In 2002 Taha Jabir Al-Alwan and the school were part of a US government investigation of Islamic organizations that were flittering money to radical Islamists terrorist organizations. Alamoudi, in 1992, while still not a nationalized American citizen, took an active part in and made large donations to the Clinton Democratic presidential campaign and emerged as President Bill Clinton's personal advisor on Islamic affairs and was appointed by President Clinton as our nations "goodwill ambassador" to the Muslim nations. This last appointment by President Clinton allowed him to travel in and out of the Middle East at the expense of the US citizens. President Clinton also appointed Alamoudi to help in the development of his new presidential program, *"Religious Expressions in Public Schools,"* which established legal jurisdiction for the ACLU to have removed Christmas celebrations, including Nativity scenes, from all American public schools. Alamoudi was a regular visitor at the White House and welcomed his photo being taken with the Clintons at several major political events and he served in many influential capacities for the Clintons during their two terms, including preparing the guest list for the first White House reception (*Iftar*) to celebrate the end of the Islamic holy month of Ramadan. While still an adviser to President and Mrs. Clinton and working on the President's ACLU special program, Alamoudi made numerous controversial public statements in reference to Hamas, claiming at a 1994 special rally held in Washington, DC that <u>Hamas</u> was not a terrorist group and that he supported booth the Hamas and Hezbollah organizations and that he was a member of the Islamic Association for Palestine, an organization that supports Hamas and was listed as one of their front organizations on the confiscated MB document. As President Clinton's second term drew to a close in the late nineties, Alamoudi sought to ensure that his own access and influence at senior levels of the US government would continue even if a Republican were to capture the White House in 2000. Alamoudi was filmed in October of 2000 not only attending an anti-Israel protest in Lafayette Square across from the White House but also being one of the speakers where he proudly declared, in English, that he supported Hamas and Hezbollah. It was also documented that he had given a large donation to the 2000 US Senate campaign of Hillary Clinton, but to secure his operative position he also provided some $20,000 to help conservative activist Grover Norquist establish a nonprofit organization called the Islamic Free Market Institute just in case the Democrats did not win the election. It was Grover Norquist who supported Almoudi to be a Muslim representative for the Bush campaign. By now Alamoudi had proven to be a very affective operative for the radical Islamist movement in America, for by now he was deeply embedded in both the Democratic and Republican political parties. At the same time that he actively worked with the Clinton, Bush, and Obama administrations and the US State

Department he was serving in various executive capacities in numerous organizations sponsored by and/or founded by the Muslim Brotherhood. For example, he served as a board member of the American Muslims for Jerusalem, founded in 1999, a strong supporter of Hamas, the Islamic Free Market Institute, the Council for the National Interest Foundation, the Interfaith Impact for Justice and Peace, the Mercy International, and the Somali Relief Fund, all of which were listed as part of the Muslim Brotherhood front organizations. He was made head of the American Task Force for Bosnia, a director of the Council on American-Islamic Relations (CAIR—America's largest Muslim civil liberties and advocacy organization), a founding trustee of the Fiqh Council of North America, a regional representative for the Islamic Society of North America, president of the Muslim Students Association of the US and Canada, secretary of the Muslim-Brotherhood-affiliated Success Foundation, and director of the Talibah International Aid Association. In order to remain active as an infiltrator in the American political scene, Alamoudi donated $3,000 to the 2002 congressional campaign of the Democratic Georgia US Congresswoman Cynthia McKinney. In September of 2003, during one of his illegal return trips to Libya, he was arrested at Heathrow Airport in London, England, for taking part in an al-Qaeda assassination plot to kill the then Crown Prince Abdulla Al Saud of Saudi Arabia, and on July 29, 2004, in a US District Court, the following criminal charges were brought against Abdurahman Muhammad Alamoudi: Criminal Case No.03-513-A

> From November 1, 1995, to on or about September 28, 2003, in the Eastern District of Virginia and elsewhere, the Defendant, ABDURAHMAN MUHAMMAD ALAMOUDI, unlawfully, knowingly,

and willfully falsified, concealed and covered up by a trick, scheme and device, material facts in matters within the jurisdiction of the Department of the Treasury; Internal Revenue Service; United States Customs Service; the Department of Justice; Immigration and Naturalization Service; and the Department of Homeland Security, agencies of the executive branch of the government of the United States. **(19)**

In a July 30, 2004 the FBI in a special press release announced that:

Alamoudi pleaded guilty this morning in a hearing before District Judge Claude M. Hilton in federal court in Alexandria, Virginia. Alamoudi pleaded guilty to three felony offenses: one count of violating the International Emergency Economic Powers Act (IEEPA), which imposes terrorism-related sanctions prohibiting unlicensed travel to and commerce with Libya; one count of false statements made in his application for naturalization; and a tax offense involving a long-term scheme to conceal from the IRS his financial transactions with Libya and his foreign bank accounts and to omit material information from the tax returns filed by his charities.

Alamoudi faces a maximum sentence of 23 years in prison, seven years of supervised release, $750,000 in fines, and revocation of his citizenship. Under the terms of the plea agreement unsealed and entered today, Alamoudi agreed that he should be sentenced under the terrorism provision of the federal sentencing guidelines. He also is required to forfeit all proceeds from his illegal dealings with Libya, which total at least $910,000, including $340,000 seized from him in the United Kingdom. Under the plea agreement, Alamoudi is also required to cooperate fully and truthfully in any and all investigations. This case is being investigated by agents of the Bureau of Immigration and Customs Enforcement, Department of Homeland Security, the Internal Revenue Service - Criminal Investigations, and the Washington Field Office of the Federal Bureau of Investigation. Assistant United States Attorney Gordon D. Kromberg and Special Assistant United States Attorney Steven P. Ward, on detail from the Tax Division of the United States Department of Justice, are prosecuting the case for the United States. **(20)**

In 2004 Alamoudi was sentenced to twenty-three years in prison for his terrorist-related activates and his confession to being an infiltrator operative for the Muslim Brotherhood/radical Islamist movement in America. Abdurrahman Alamoudi was able to infiltrate and become a very influential operative from 1985 to 2003. The Divine Law, Shari'ah law, ordains lying to nonbelievers is permissible without accountability and retribution, known as *al-taqiyya* in Islam. Al-Taqiyya allows an individual to conceal or disguise their beliefs and convictions, which allows them to be excellent infiltrators. How much strategic classified information and damage was Alamoudi able to inflict on America's national security? The important factor here is that Alamoudi is only one of thousands of such operatives still actively working within America. Why would the President, who took an oath to protect America and its citizens, try several times to have this individual, who admitted to and was found guilty of trying to destroy the very country he swore to protect, have Alamoudi freed from prison? **(21)**

A question Americans and the American government need to ask is **who** is Saeed Abedini, an individual with dual Iran/American citizenship who converted from Islam to become a Christian pastor in America and an individual who was one of the Americans exchanged for Iranian terrorist prisoners as part of the Iran Nuclear deal between Iran and America in 2016. According to the Qur'an in Surat 9:66: *"apostasy in Islam is worse than being an infidel"* and they are to *"pay the ultimate price with no leniencies."* How and why did Saeed Abedini, a publically declared apostate by converting from Islam to Christianity, survive as a prisoner in the strict Islamic county of Iran and be sent safely back to America as part of a prisoner exchange? **Who** is Saeed Abedini? **Why** did the Islamic state of Iran not obey their obligations of Allah and Muhammad nor that of Shari'ah law, and not make him *"pay the ultimate price with no leniencies"* for *"apostasy in Islam is worse than being an infidel"* but instead send him back to America as an exchange prisoner?

The strategy behind such an implemented and carefully placed individual was to sabotage America's strengths, weaknesses, and vulnerabilities. This was accomplished by attacking and weakening its citizen's values systems, beliefs, emotions, reasoning, and decision-making capabilities and threatening their conscious and subconscious mind-sets (attitudes and feelings), their fear factors, and their sense of security. To do true justice to the topic of the extent of compromising infiltration into the American infrastructure would take another book. I recommend the reading of the Muslim Brotherhood's strategic plan for North America document, "An Explanatory Memorandum: On the General Strategic Goal for the Group," that was discovered by the FBI during the arrest and raid of the residence of Ismael Selim Elbarasse in Annandale, Virginia. It is worth reading as it clearly defines their mission for infiltrating North America in what they refer to as:

> The process of settlement is a "Civilization-Jihadist Process" with all the word means. The Ikhwan must understand that their work in America is a kind of grand jihad in eliminating and destroying the Western civilization from within and "sabo-taging" its miserable house by their hands and the hands of the believers so that it is eliminated and God's religion is made victorious over all other religions. **(22)**

Abdul Rahman al-Almoudi is only one example of how effective and well organized the Muslim Brotherhood commitment to *"The process of settlement is a 'Civilization-Jihadist Process' "* of placing a very dedicated radical Islamist member of the MB into very influential government positions, including the office of the president of the United States and the US State Department. The question that the American citizens and its government officials need to ask is: from what type of individuals do they, the radical Islamist, select and draw their recruits and support from?

The radical Islamist use of psychological warfare is staged to portray the role of the terrorist as heroic and being a strong bond of brotherhood. Even their staged and recorded acts of savagery have proven to be an effective double strategy as they have been an effective recruiting tool and secondly they have generated fear in the minds and hearts of Jews, Christians, and Muslims throughout the world. Their warfare strategy in the infiltration, into America's infrastructure has proven their ability to incite and control revolts and public uprisings, the nation's media, and the undercurrents in the very foundation of the citizens' guaranteed freedoms. The important factor in evaluating their strategic use of psychological warfare is not only to consider who their targeted audience is but also how they target their audiences' vulnerabilities, such as their government officials, their media, their social structure, and their general public. It is important to understand that **psychological warfare is not an end in itself, but a means to an end.** After liberating a *Dar-al-Harb* country from its nonbelievers, the radical Islamist seeks to establish an Islamic state according to the prophetic model of Muhammad established by the Hijrah of the seventh century. It is because of the major influence that Prophet Muhammad's 622 AD Hijrah has on how and why the twenty-first century radical Islamist movement is so committed and so effective in their use of psychological warfare that I have dedicated a full chapter to the subject.

FOOTNOTES:

1. Hassan al-Banna founder of the Muslim Brotherhood and the key individual quoted often by the twenty-first century radical Islamic Jihadist.

2. Ibn Khaldean, (1332-1406), _Muqaddimah- An Introduction to History – The Classic Islamic History of the World,_ Princeton University Press, 1967.

3. Sahih-Bukhari, _Hadith,_ Volume 7, Book 67, Number 427, Narrated by Zahdam. http://www.sahih-bukhari.com/Pages/Bukhari_72/45 php. (Retrieved 4/2/2017)

4. Newt Gingrich, The Wall Street Journal, January 15, 2015.

5. Sahih Bukhari, _Hadith,_ Book 52, Number 269, Narrated Jabir bin 'Abdullah, http://www.sahih-bukhari.com/Pages/Bukhari_52/269 php. (Retrieved 3/24/2017)

6. Eric Hoffer, 1951, _'The True Believer: Thoughts on the Nature of Mass Movements'_ , Harper Publishers. I required all of my graduate students studying terrorism to be familiar with Eric Hoffer.

7. Paraphrased from manuscript, Abu Bakr Naji, The _Management of Savager: The Most Critical Stage Through Which the Ummah Will Pass._ Translated from the Arabic by William McCants, a fellow at West Point's Harmony Project -Combating Terrorism Center. https://www.ctc.usma.edu/programs-resources/harmony-program. (Retrieved 4/02/2017)

8. Ibid. Abu Bakr Naji.

9. Abu Bakr Naji, there have been many speculations to his true nationality, authored , *The Management of Savagery*, which has been quoted numerous time by various radical Islamist publications and posted in its entirety on the al-Qaeda internet Sawt al-Jihad. It is the most published work to be found today. The exact date of its publication is not known but it appeared on the al-Qaeda Internet magazine in 2004 and has become widely quoted since then.

10. Eric Hoffer, 1951, *The True Believer: Thoughts on the Nature of Mass Movements,* Harper Publishers.

11. Chairman Mao-Tse-Tung, January 27, 1934), Selected Works, Vol. I, p. 147.

12. Ibid. Chairman Mao-Tse-Tung.

13. Muslim Brotherhood, "Phased Plan," dated May 22, 1991, a document entered into evidence in the US vs Holy Land Foundation, *Shariah—The Threat to America —An Exercise in Competitive Analysis p Report Team BII*, The Security for Security Policy, Washington, D.C., pg. 273. **And** http://www. investigativeproject.org/document/20-an-explanatory-memorandum- -on-the-general.pdf (Retrieved 3/23/2017)

14. Sun Tsu, *The Art of War,* Chartwell Books, 2012, *and* Translated by Lionel Giles Original Text.)

15. Ibid, Muslim Brotherhood, *An Explanatory Memorandum on the General Strategic Goal for the Group in North America.*

16. Ibid. Muslim Brotherhood, An Explanatory Memorandum on the General Strategic Goal for the Group in North America.

17. Ibid, Muslim Brotherhood, An Explanatory Memorandum on the General Strategic Goal for the Group in North America. US vs. Holy Land Foundation document Bate # ISE-SW 1823/U002005.

18. US District Court for the Eastern District of Virginia, Alexandra Division vs. Abdurahman Muhammad Alamoudi, Criminal No. 03-513-A. July 29, 2004, http://www.investigativeproject.org/documents/case_docs/220.pdf. (Retrieved 1/23/2017)

19. US vs. Holy Land Foundation document Bate # ISE-SW 1823/U002005.

20. The Federal Bureau of Investigation, *U.S. Announces Plea in Terrorism Financing Case - U.S. Citizen Agrees to Plead Guilty to Criminal Violations Including Violating Anti-Terrorism Sanctions Law, Washington, D.C. July 30, 2004.*

21. President Barak Obama before leaving the end of his second presidential term in 2016-2017.

22. Mohamed Akram, May 19, 1991, *An Explanatory Memorandum on the General Strategic Goal for the Brotherhood in North America, Government Exhibit 003-0085, 2:04-CR-204-G, U.S. vs HLF, et. Al.*

VI
CONCLUSION

"And those who disbelieve and deny Our signs—those will be companions of the Fire; they will abide therein eternally." The Holy Qur'an, Surat 2:39

The answers to the four questions listed below are found throughout the previous five chapters:

(Q1) Why has the radical Islamist targeted and declared war against America?

(Q2) Why are America and other Western nations experiencing an increase in 'homegrown' or also referred to as the 'lone wolf' terrorists?

(Q3) What is the ultimatum they are demanding?

(Q4) Why are their acts of violence and carnage against not only the military but also against the nation's non-military innocent citizens?

Invariably during one of my lectures or even during a casual conversation someone will ask one or all four of these questions and expect a three- or four-word response. That is impossible but in this final chapter I shall endeavor to point out the key factors that have been defined in the previous chapters that answer these four noted questions. As I stated in the introduction, my intentions in writing this book were not only to explain why the radical Islamists do what they do but to prove why they do what they do based on their use of (1) the three most sacred texts of Islam; (2) the scholarly rhetoric quoted by and used regularly by the radical Islamists Sheikh Hassan al-Banna, Al-Shaheed Sayyid Qutb, and Abdullah Yusuf Assam; (3) the important radical Islamist documents confiscated during intelligence raids and used as evidence in several court trials; and (4) their international propaganda media coverage. With that said, let us begin our journey in answering the above four strategic and frequently asked questions.

I need to clarify why I have chosen only the literary rhetoric from three radical Islamist scholars. Much rhetoric has been expressed about the glory and historical importance of the seventh century and the first Islamic ummah and their great conquests under the leadership of the Prophet Muhammad. Using Muhammad as their role model and the courage and undeniable allegiance of his converts/warriors Sheikh Hassan al-Banna, Al-Shaheed Sayyid Qutb and Abdullah Yusuf Assam has been perhaps the most influential in providing answers to these four questions. All three scholars have been dramatically influential as reactionary motivators and are recognized as the "Grandfathers of the twenty-first century Global Jihad." By defining their influence as being "dramatically influential as reactionary motivators" I am stressing the undeniable large extent and the impressive manner in which these three men have influenced the lives and the extreme behavior of the twenty-first century radical Islamist. Their literary rhetoric is often quoted during Friday sermons, international media coverage, fatwas, staged propaganda videos, and media postings and are part of their training manuals. All three men were prominent leaders in the Muslim Brotherhood organization and believed and promoted that all Muslims are obligated to fight in a Jihad (war) to spread Islam throughout the world—a Global Jihad against the "*enemies of Islam.*"

(Q1) Why has the radical Islamist targeted and declared war against America?

Sheikh Al-Shaheed Sayyid Qutb, successor to al-Banna as leader of the Muslim Brotherhood and author, poet, and Islamic theorist, had a pronounced influence on the revival of the radical Islamists, their ideology based on religion, their call for a Global Jihad, and their hatred for America based partly on his opinion of the Western culture following his visit and tenure in America on an Egyptian student fellowship. In his most famous literary work **Milestones Along the Road** (Ma'alim fi al-T of ariq) he described the decline in the "*Western culture,*" an opinion that is shared by the radical Islamist and many individuals including some Americans:

> The leadership of mankind by Western man is now on the decline, not because Western culture has become poor materially or because its economic and military power has become weak. The period of the Western system has come to an end primarily because it is deprived of those

life-giving values which enabled it to be the leader of mankind. **(1)**

Qutb established the mode among these young mujahidin that
America was on its decline and was weak and vulnerable. It was
because of such statements as noted above, combined with his
strong beliefs and charismatic leadership of the largest and the
oldest and most aggressive radical Islamist movement, that Qutb
had a powerful influence on Muslims throughout the world. He
reinforced the idea that the second super power country in the
world, America, was ready to be infiltrated and destroyed from
within. A project that has been proven to still be alive, active,
and effective in the twenty-first century in America. Chapter
I, "Revival of the Radical Islamist: The Muslim Brotherhood"
describes how the Muslim Brotherhood organization had
incorporated into the American infrastructure a ***"Civilization
Jihad Settlement Process for eliminating and destroying the
Western civilization from within and 'sabotaging' its miserable
house by their own hands"*** **(2)**. It was Qutb's strong disapproval
and ridicule of America, plus his division of the world as being
only two entities, ***Dar-al-Islam***, the land or abode of Islam, and
Dar-al-Harb, the land or abode of war (nonbelievers), good
versus evil, both found within his book ***Milestones Along the
Road*** that made America an ***"enemy of Islam"***:

> **Only one place on earth can be called the home
> of Islam (Dar-al-Islam), and that is the place
> where the Islamic state is established and the
> Shari'ah is enforced and Allah's limits are ob-
> served** and where all the Muslims administer the
> affairs of the community with mutual consulta-
> tion. **(3)**

And the rest of world is:

> **The rest of the world is the home of hostility (Dar-al-Harb). A Muslim can have only two possible relations with Dar-al-Harb: peace with a contractual agreement, or war. (4)**

This one statement clearly provided the radical Islamist a full blueprint for why they have such profound hostility toward America, the Western European nations, and any nation which they have designated as being in the land of war. Sayyid Qutb set the boundaries by which the present radical Islamists justify their violence against both Muslims and non-Muslim, for, "Only one place on earth can be called the home of Islam (Dar-al-Islam), and that is the place where the Islamic state is established and the Shari'ah is enforced and Allah's limits are observed." America is not a nation in which its executive, legislative, and judicial branches are dictated by its nation's religious beliefs and/or the Divine Laws of Allah—Shari'ah law. No one can deny that America, according to Qutb's division of the world and Allah's revelation found in Surat 5:47: **"Let the People of the Gospel judge by what Allah hath revealed therein. If any do fail to Judge by what hath revealed they are those who rebel."** And/or *Surat 2:39 "But they who disbelieve, and deny our revelations, such are rightful Peoples of the Fire. They will abide therein."* Muhammad, peace be upon him, informed his followers: "Oh you who believe! Take not my enemies And your enemies as friends offering them (Your) love even though they have disbelieved in that Truth (i.e. Allah, Prophet Muhammad and this Qur'an) which has come to you" **(5).** The radical Islamists put their trust in the literary words of

Sayyid Qutb, the revelations found in the Holy Qur'an, and the directions of Muhammad found in the Sunnah/Hadith.

The radical Islamists have voiced many grievances, either real or propaganda, against America and the American government and its citizens. These grievances have been used to exploit and reveal America's vulnerabilities and weaknesses and to establish numerous reasons why they should attack and destroy America. By numerous propaganda ploys they have been able to prove to thousands of Islamists that **"America is an enemy of Islam."** Qutb's influence and doctrine, known as *Qutbism,* on the future radical Islamist generations can be noted in the 1996 and 1998 declarations of war issued against America by Usama bin Laden, then leader of the al-Qaeda international terrorist organization. The first declaration, published in August of 1996, was addressed to and titled a *"Declaration of War Against the Americans Occupying the Land of the Two Holy Places,"* and was issued and signed only by Usama bin Mohammed bin Awad bin Laden himself; however, the second declaration, published on February 23, 1998, was addressed and titled *"Declaration of the **World Islamic Front for Jihad** against the Jews and the Crusaders"* and was issued and signed not only by Shaykh Usama Bin-Muhammad Bin-Laden (leader of the al-Qaeda international terrorist organization) but also Ayman al-Zawahiri (Amir of the Jihad Group in Egypt), Abu- Yasir Rifa'i Ahmad Taha,(a leader of the [Egyptian] Islamic Group), Shaykh Mir Hamzah (secretary of the Jamiat-al-Ulema of Pakistan), and Fazlul Rahman (Amir of the Jihad Movement in Bangladesh). What a strategic physiological act, for by the additional supporters' signatures bin Laden made a powerful statement to both the *Dar al-Islam* (the world of Islam and believers) and to the *Dar-al-Harb* (the world of war and nonbelievers) that his declaration of war was now a Global Jihad. Both declarations stated many propaganda grievances to gather world-wide sympathy even from American citizens. Bin Laden's first accusation is that America is attacking the Muslim universal um-mah (community) because of its support of the creation of Israel and the Israelis' continued aggression against the people of Palestine. With this one statement America was automatically made an *"enemy of Islam."* I was reminded during one of my trips to the Middle East: "The United states and your president were the first to acknowledge and approve Israel as a Jewish nation." This is true as President Truman was the first head of state in the world to acknowledge Israel as an independent nation and America was the first nation in the UN to nominate Israel to be accepted as a sovereign nation. Within minutes of America's nomination of Israel as a sovereign independent nation the am-bassador to the UN from Russia seconded the motion and voted Russia's approval. This one incident has left an open wound, still, in the twenty-first century, in the hearts and mind-set of many Arabs and Muslims throughout the world. One must remember that this enormous decision was made without the consent and/or votes of any Arab and/or Muslim nation. Another accusation that has become a powerful recruiting tool for the radical Islamist movement stresses the vulnerability and weakness found within America's military history by the citing of their 1993 attack against Americas Special Forces in Somalia, forcing them to retreat and return to America. This one small portion of the declaration sent the message that if the Mujahidin were committed to the cause of *Dar-al-Islam* and willing to perform violent acts of carnage that their enemy *Dar-al-Harb* would retreat and be beaten. This same rhetoric was noted in Friday morning sermons and in media pro-paganda in reference to our retreating from Iraq and Afghanistan because of the Mujahidin's violent and unrestrained fighting against the American military forces. Another noted propaganda grievance in bin Laden's declarations of war that gained sympathy and support throughout the world was the false accusation that *"more than 1.5 million Iraqi children have died as a result of your (America) sanction"* **(6).** The sanctions bin Laden was referring to, *"oil for food,"* was imposed by the United Nations Security Council which stated that 70 percent of Iraq's sale of oil had to be used for humanitarian supplies for the people of Iraq. Unfortunately, the United Nations did not establish a check-and-balance system to monitor Iraq's compliance to the program and as various investigative commissions found later, the money, estimated to be about $67 billion in revenues between 1997 and 2002, had been squandered by Saddam Hussein and his government and by the then President of the United Nations Kofi Annan and his son. As with numerous data and grievances, bin Laden's figures were vastly overly exaggerated as were those reported by the United Nations Development Program, UNICEF, the Ministry of Iraqi Health, and the World Health Organization original reports which they each retracted, and they admitted that their figures included combatants and figures quoted by Iraqi government officials and were not accurate. Unfortunately many Americans including the media based their opinions and reporting on the false statements made by various not-creditable and not-accurate surveys. Numerous accusations were featured in both Declarations of War issued by bin Laden and other radical Islamist leaders; they can be downloaded from the Internet at Harmony Program, Combating Terrorism Center at West Point. There is one major grievance that, found in both declarations, requires special attention for it accused America of occupying "our countries; you spread your military bases throughout them; you corrupt our lands, and you besiege our sanctities, to protect the security of the Jews and to ensure the continuity of your pillage of our treasures and turning its bases in the Peninsula into a spearhead through which to fight the neighboring Muslim peoples" (7). Americans, including some of our government officials, seem to have focused on this one issue as the true major reason for al-Qaeda's and the radical Islamists attacks against Americans and hence demanded that we remove all of the American military personnel and its equipment from the Middle East region. I have heard many Americans state *"that if we pull our troops out of Saudi Arabia and the Middle East region the terrorists will not attack our nation or its citizens ever again. The terrorists will leave us alone!"* Unfortunately this grievance made by the radical Islamists against America became part of a strong presidential campaign platform promise in the 2008 and 2012 elections that proved to help win many votes. In keeping with his campaign promise, the president, acting as commander in chief of the military, started pulling American personnel out of Afghanistan, Iraq, and Saudi Arabia. The demobilization was completed on December 18, 2011. The important proven facts are (1) the removal of US military presence in the Middle East had **NO** bearing on nor any influence on the attacks against America and its citizens. American citizens are still being targeted, killed, and wounded by the radical Islamists in Algeria, Australia, America, Brussels, Canada, Denmark, Great Britain, Egypt, France, Indonesia, Kenya, Spain, and Tunisia. But (2) **IT DID** allow the radical Islamists to regroup, increase their number of mujahidin, and surge and victimize Muslims and non-Muslims in Afghanistan, Algeria, Bangladesh, Egypt, Iraq, Kuwait, Lebanon, Libya, Philippines, Saudi Arabia, Syria, Turkey, and Yemen. The bottom line is the American citizens who volunteered and sacrificed their lives to provide peace and security to the citizens of Afghanistan and Iraq and the United States died for nothing because al-Qaeda in Iraq became ISIS and al-Qaeda/Taliban have retaken control of the region and are victimizing, torturing, and killing innocent citizens, whether they be Muslims and/or non-Muslims and have now extended that threat throughout the world. **(3) IT PROVED,** to the Islamist mujahidin and the Muslim ummah, that bin Laden was correct for when America is threatened and attacked it will pull its military out and run and not defend its honor nor its word just like it did in Somalia. In reference to part of this quoted grievance is the claim that the American military troops have occupied designated military bases for support and housing within the Middle East region. This is true but unlike al-Qaeda, ISIS, and the radical Islamist terrorist guerilla movements who established their bases within Middle East nations by brutal force and horrendous acts of carnage, the American military was invited with the support of the host country. Both of bin Laden's 1996 and 1998 declarations were written following *"Operation Desert Storm"* or as often referred to as the *"Gulf War,"* in which a coalition was made up of thirty-nine nations including ten Muslim, of which six were Arab/Muslim nations and all were under a special coalition formed by the United Nations. For the record, the thirty-nine UN coalition consisted of the nations of Afghanistan, Argentina, Australia, Bahrain, Bangladesh, Belgium, Canada, Czechoslovakia, Denmark, Egypt, France, Germany, Greece, Honduras, Hungry, Italy, Netherlands, New Zealand, Niger, Norway, Oman, Pakistan, Poland, Portugal, Qatar, Romania, Saudi Arabia, Senegal, Sierra Leone, Singapore, South Korea, Spain, Sweden, Syria, Turkey, the United Kingdom, the United Arab Emirates, and the United States. However, the declarations were declared only against the American military forces *"Occupying the Land of the Two Holy Places,"* and not against any of the other thirty-eight nations. The military bases, on holy soil, that bin Laden is alluding to housed and supported a total of 670,000 military personnel, of which 450,000 were US personnel. The United States, at the request of the Saudi Arabian and the

Kuwait monarchies and under the mandate issued by the United Nations, was made the supreme commander of one the largest international allied military coalitions. Any successful military operation, especially when coordinating 670,000 combat personnel from twenty-three different nations, can only function by having one principal commander in position to establish order and direct leadership. Each of the coalitions' military divisions had commanders in charge of their individual personnel and who were part of the military decision-making process. General Dwight Eisenhower held the position of Supreme Allied Commander in WWII for the allied forces; bin Laden held that position for multinational al-Qaeda terrorist organizations, Ayatollah Khomeini for the Iranian Revolution, Hitler for the Axis in WW II. Each of these noted accusations and my documented responses are perfect examples of how true the young Arab's statement "The United States are so easy to influence and infiltrate, they will believe any form of grievances you bring against them and feel sorry for you even when it is not true and when you have murdered their own citizens" really was and how gullible and vulnerable the American citizens, their elected representatives, and its social media are to the radical Islamist propaganda. These two declarations of war validated Sayyid Qutb's statement that the world was divided into two entices: *Dar-al-Islam* and *Dar-al-Harb* for the radical Islamist and clearly designated America as being an *enemy of Islam* and therefore in the *Dar-al-Harb* – the abode of war. They also were warnings of what America could expect in the future from its self-declared enemy—the global radical Islamist movement.

Why America? In addition to Qutb's division of the world into *Dar-al-Islam* and *Dar-al-Harb* supported by the revelations of Allah and the words of the prophet Muhammad, peace be upon him, and the various grievances noted in the two Declarations of War against America, are the numerous challenges the Western modernization and technology has forced on the traditional Islamic order. Their greatest challenge has been the humiliation and shame that this modernization and technology brought to their region and nations. With the invention of mass technology and the advancement of Western modernization the world saw how underdeveloped and unprogressive the Arab/Muslim nations actually were. Modern technology and advancement did not actually occur within this region until the mid and or late 1990s and some of these regions still in 2017 lack any form of modernization. News coverage of the wars in Iraq and Afghanistan after 9/11 revealed to the world the villages and whole regions in which the citizens were living in mud houses or no houses with no running water, no electricity, no healthcare facilities, and/or no secular education facilities. The radical Islamists have fought modernization and advanced technology in their regions because of their beliefs in (1) **traditionalism** in which they defend their (2) **religious ideology** and their (3) **Islamic historical visions** of a universal Islamic ummah as that founded by Muhammad in the seventh century. Remember, humiliation and shame is not something that the Arab/Muslim culture can easily ascribe to. The radical Islamists want to return Islam to its pure historical Golden Age by the use of modern technology and warfare. A declared Global Jihad war against all forms of modernization which they have judged to be *"enemies of Islam."* That is their dilemma!

Why America? My personal belief is that their claimed grievances and fight against modernization and technology, except if they can be used as tools for war, are forms of propaganda to enhance their demand for sympathy and personal pride. History reveals how heroes always need a cause and then someone to blame that cause on. Why? Because the cause could never be a fault of their own. Adolf Hitler is a perfect example of this mind-set and psychological warfare strategy. I believe their strategy to attack and declare war against America as a major part of their Global Jihad, as noted throughout this book, is actually based on their prime strategy that if America as a super power can be conquered and declared Islam under Shari'ah law, then the rest of the nations that make up the non-Muslim world will crumble also. Prior to the 1979 war between Afghanistan and the Soviet Union, the world in their eyes consisted of two super powers: America and the Soviet Union, and with the fall of the Soviet Union one super power had been destroyed by the radical Islamic movement, a movement that was only powerful because once again the Muslim global ummah had come together to fight an enemy of Allah—the atheist Soviet Union. This one victory proved to the radical Islamists that they had won the favor of Allah and were true *"warriors of Allah."* America is judged to be an "enemy of Islam," the same as the Soviet Union had been prejudged by the radicals Islamic leaders. With the fall of the Soviet Union, fifteen separate nations were formed and out of those fifteen nations nine are predominately Muslim in the twenty-first century. A bit of trivia: in the 2008 Olympics held in Beijing, China, the Russian Olympic team won twenty-three gold medals, ten of which were won by Russian indigenous Muslim athletes. Many people do not realize that the Islamic conquest entered into the Russian territory in the mid seventh century and these people became part of the Russian Federation. America is a threat to the radical Islamic movement on two strategic fronts: first as a superpower nation that holds a definite economic influence in the world and because it has one of the strongest and most advanced military forces; and second because America is definitely a nation that lives in the abode of war, *Dar-al-Harb*, because it is a nation made up of nonbelievers and is not ruled under the Divine Laws of Allah—Shari'ah law. The radical Islamists are betting on their strategy that if they can force the fall of America then the Middle East and European nations that are allies of America will crumble also - a strategy that I believe they have been working on since 1979.

(Q2) Why are America and other Western nations experiencing an increase in 'homegrown' or also referred to as the 'lone wolf' terrorists?

Imam Hassan al-Banna, the founder and leader of the world's most influential radical Islamist organization, the *Muslim Brotherhood,* made the following statements in his most famous reactionary motivational book titled **The Way of Jihad: The Complete Text by Hassan Al-Banna founder of the Muslim Brotherhood**: "Jihad is an obligation from Allah on every Muslim and cannot be ignored or evaded and furthermore Allah has specifically honored the mujahidin with certain exceptional qualities, both spiritual and practical, to benefit them in this world and the next. " This one statement has served as a calling card to young Muslims from around the world and answers the question as to why there has been an increase in homegrown or lone-wolf terrorists in America and throughout the world. The homegrown Islamic terrorist ideology is based on the same religious concepts as the members of ISIS, al-Qaeda, and the Muslim Brotherhood organizations. They have to be connected to some belief and organized strategy in order to be indoctrinated, recruited, and trained and to be able to plan their acts of violence, indoctrinated into a **Blind Submission and Allegiance** to the overall doctrine that is leading the movement.

Why? Because authoritarianism is imbedded in their thought as they see themselves as *"warriors of Allah"* and as such they are part of the Islamic movement to *"purify the soul of Islam."*

The Qur'an performs two functions in the ideology of the radical Islamist: first it is the undeniable authority of Allah and secondly it ensures and preserves Allah's message for all mankind. Therefore, verses in the Qur'an such as 9:123 **"O ye who believe! Fight the unbelievers who are near to you and let them find harshness in you: and know that Allah is with those who fear Him"** and 4:84 **"Then fight in Allah's cause— thou are held responsible accountable only for thyself- and rouse the believers. It may be that Allah will restrain the fury of the Unbelievers; for Allah is the strongest in might and in punishment."** The two previous quotes and 5:33 and 47:4 each make it clear that it is an obligation of all Muslims to fight and destroy all nonbelievers. The authorization of the Qur'an and the Sunnah/Hadith is imbedded into their mindset. In other words, for the radial Islamist as *"warriors of Allah"* acting individually or as part of group they are still obligated and justified in committing any act of violence against anyone who has been judged to be a nonbeliever and/or living in the abode of war—*Dar-al-Harb*.

For young Muslims throughout the world, including the United States, bin Laden's messages found in the 1996 and 1998 issued *"Documents of War against America"* made an indebted mark and called for all Muslims to join the fight against the advocating supremacy of the Americans and their allies **(8). Both declarations not only served as "declarations of war" but they also were warnings of what America could expect in the future from its self-declared enemy**—the global radical Islamist movement—and they incited young radicals throughout the world that they were obligated to join and fight for the cause.

(Q3) What is the ultimatum they are demanding?

The three historical literary scholars known as the "*Grandfathers of the twenty-first century Global Jihad*' have each expressed what is the ultimatum the radical Islamists are demanding: (1) Hassan al-Banna made the following statement that has been quoted and has influenced radical Islamists throughout the world: **"It is the nature of Islam to dominate, not to be dominated, to impose its law on all nations and to extend its power to the entire planet" (9).** (2) Sayyid Qutb made the following statement as to what the radical Islamists want: **"If Islam is again to play the role of the leader of mankind, then it is necessary that the Muslim community be restored to its original form."** For, **"Islam is the only System that possesses these values and this way of life" (10).** (3) Shaikh 'Abdullah Yusuf 'Azzam, famous Islamist literary writer for his militant interpretation of the Islamic doctrine of '*Jihad* and *co*founder of al-Qaeda made the following statement: ***"Jihad* must not be abandoned until Allah alone is worshipped. *Jihad* continues until Allah's Word is raised high. *Jihad* until all the oppressed peoples are freed. *Jihad* to protect our dignity and restore our occupied lands. *Jihad* is the way of everlasting glory" (11).** The answer to this question has also been clearly stated in both declarations of war declared by bin Laden and issued in 1996 and in 1998: **"*The first thing that we are calling you to is Islam"* (12).** One must understand that there is no either/ or and no leverage for negations! This one statement should have been a wakeup call for all Americans and especially to our government's national security organization, and yet no one considered it important enough to even address. Even the media washed over it and yet it is the prime reason for their declarations of war and their call for a Global Jihad. WHY? For the radical Islamist, as stated in the Qur'an and the Sunnah/ Hadith, there is only one *"true religion"* and that is the religion of Islam. This war is not about the various declared grievances but rather about establishing a universal Islamic world under one law—Shari'ah law.

> (a) The religion of the Unification of God; of free-dom from associating partners with Him, and rejection of this; of complete love of Him, the Exalted; **of complete submission to His Laws;** and of the discarding of all the opinions, orders, theories and religions which contradict with the religion He sent down to His Prophet Muhammad (peace be upon him). Islam is the religion of all the prophets, and makes no distinction between them—peace be upon them all. **It is to this religion that we call you; the seal of all the previous religions. It is the religion of Unification of God.** **(13)**

The above quote from the 1996 declaration clearly states in black and white, with no gray areas, that the only way this war can end is if the American citizens and its **government agree to become Muslims and agree to accept and follow Shari'ah law.** **"It is to this religion that we call you; the seal of all the previous religions. It is the religion of Unification of God. It is the religion of enjoining the good and forbidding the evil with the hand, tongue, and heart."** And he added that **"the Qur'an is the miracle until the Day of Judgment."** Why would the American government and its citizens reject such demands which were so clearly defined and expressed by the enemy who had declared war against its nation and citizens? **For the radical Islamist, the final conclusion is that America and the world will become part of the universal Muslim ummah or the world will come to an end, whichever comes first**. In Chapter IV "Fighting for the Soul of Islam: Global Jihad," I quoted from various Quranic and Sunnah/Hadith sacred messages which revealed the blueprint and justification for what they are demanding from America and the world in order to stop this war, which they declared in 1979 with the deliberate attack on the American Embassy and the holding of fifty-two American citizens as hostages in Iran.

How many innocent lives were lost before the world finally accepted and believed Hitler's statements and declarations of war? Like Hitler, our enemy has told us exactly what they have demanded of us and what winning this war means to them. Hitler, in his autobiography, written while he was in prison and before he became Fuhrer, describes his plans, his mind-set, and his ideology. As an American I can honestly say we, as a nation, do not learn from history and we have a pattern of repeating ourselves no matter how tragic or how devastating the results may be. The British had demanded that the Americans give up their claims of independence and remain under their dictatorship, which resulted in the American Revolution (1775–1783). Our forefathers went up against the world's most disciplined and equipped armed military and navy fleet in the world at that time. It was a war fought so that each of us would have the right to choose our own religion and live in a land free of a dictatorship and an opportunity to better our lives and that of our children and future generations. I ask you, the reader, the same final exam question I always asked my students in my graduate courses: "Which constitutional right are you willing to sacrifice in order to guarantee your children, your grandchildren, and future generations the type of nation that so many Americans have sacrificed their lives for, including our forefathers, and one which you enjoyed and experienced as a child"? My students always responded that it was one of the most difficult questions they ever had to answer—but they all answered the question. For the radical Islamist mujahidin, their fighting for a universal Islamic world is an obligation dictated by Allah in his revelations. As warriors in a Global Jihad, if they win or if they die they will be honored by Allah, the Islamic universal ummah, their family, and their fellow mujahidin. What a powerful recruiting tool for this generation and for generations to follow to be given the opportunity and the ability to fight and die for Allah and to establish a world under the only one pure religion—"*the seal of all the previous religions,*" and "*it is the religion of Unification of God*"—Islam.

(Q4) Why are their acts of violence and carnage against not only the military but also against the nation's nonmilitary innocent citizens?

Abdulla Azzam has been criticized for justifying the killing of civilians deemed *mushrikeen* (polytheists) in Jihad, telling mujahidin that the enemies of Islam: ***"They seek to extinguish the light of Allah by their mouths. But Allah refuses save to perfect His light, even if the Disbelievers are averse. It is He who has sent His messenger with the guidance and the true religion, in order that He may make it prevail over all religions, even if the pagans are averse"*** *(Qur'an, 9:32-33).* Bin Laden in his declarations of war answered the question as to why the radical Islamists would be justified in killing innocent citizens: "because you pay taxes that support the policies and because the American people are the ones who choose their government by way of their own free will; a choice which stems from their agreement to its policies" **(14).** Allah's Apostle Muhammad, peace be upon him, stated that he had been ordered by Allah to fight against all the nonbelievers: "I have been ordered (by Allah) to fight against the people until they testify that none has the right to be worshipped but Allah and that Muhammad is Allah's Apostle" **(15).** All individuals are deemed guilty who live in the abode or house of war until **"they *testify that none has the right to be worshiped but Allah according to the sacred Qur'an."* Even innocent citizens, are guilty by association rather than by any crime that they have committed. Literary scholars and radical Islamist leaders have quoted both the Qur'an and the Sunnah/Hadith to justify their horrendous acts of violence against innocent citizens, such as Surat 3, verse 85: *"If anyone desires a religion other than Islam (submission to God), never will it be accepted of him; and in the Hereafter he will be in the ranks of those who have lost All spiritual good."* (Surat 3:85 abrogates, or eliminates, 2:246, 2:256 and 257.) The Prophet Muhammad, peace be upon him, "was asked if it was permissible to attack the pagan warriors at night with the probability of exposing their women and children to danger. The Prophet replied, 'They (i.e. women and children) are from them (i.e. pagans)" **(16).** "And I heard the Prophet saying, 'The institution of Hima is invalid except for Allah and His Apostle.'" If the parents were infidels, then it is permissible to kill their children. For the radical Islamists who have pledged their allegiance to Muhammad and believe him to be their perfect role model, if the prophet ordained it then it automatically became a command for them.

Muslims believe that the revelations found in the Qur`an consist of words that were miraculously placed in the heart of the Prophet Muhammad by Allah. Therefore a major part of being Muslim is to pledge your undeniable allegiance to Muhammad as the Messenger of God and to have total submission to Allah. For the radical Islamist, Muhammad has been ordained by Allah as the last prophet for the world, not just for the Muslims but for all mankind. Therefore not just America but the world must submit to Islam and the Divine Laws of Allah for "It is the nature of Islam to dominate, not to be dominated, to impose its law on all nations and to extend its power to the entire planet." The two most influential sources of Islamic knowledge are the Qur'an and the Sunnah/Hadith, which I have used throughout this book to add credibility and clarification. The Qur'an and the Sunnah are the embodiment of justice and the Shari'ah is the mechanism to enforce that justice. For the radical Islamist, Shari'ah law is the only answer to a perfect world order.

"Allah is our objective. The Prophet is our leader. Qur'an is our law. *Jihad* is our way. Dying in the way of Allah is our highest hope." Motto of the Muslim Brotherhood and it should also be the motto for the radical Islamist movement.

NOTES:

1. Al Shaheed Sayyid Quib, 1964, 'Milestones Along the Road' (Ma'alim fi al-T of ariq), Azzam Publications; 2nd, Revised edition May 1, 2001 (retrieved 6/11/2017) ttp://www.kalam-ullah.com/Books/milestones.pdf.) Sayyid Qutb, "Milestone Along the Road, (Ma'alim fi al-Tariq) Chapter IX—A Muslim's Nationality and Belief.

2. "An Explanatory Memorandum on the General Strategic Goal for the Group in North America," Government Exhibit 003-0085 3:04-CR-240-G. https://www.justice.gov/opa/pr/federal-judge-hands-downs-sentences-holy-land-foundation-case (Retrieved 9/23/2017)

3. Ibid. Al Shaheed Sayyid Qutb, "Milestones".

4. Ibid. Al Shaheed Sayyid Qutb, "Milestones".

5. Sahih Bukhari, Vol 5, Book 59, Hadith 572, narrated by 'Ali.

6. Bin Laden's "1996 Declaration of War Against US" : Script taken from Fatwa found in Archives West Point. https://www.usma.edu/library/sitepages/sca.aspx. (Retrieved 6/10/2017)

7. Ibid. Bin Laden, "1996 Declaration of War Against US".

8. Both of these documents can be downloaded from the internet at Harmony Program, Combating Terrorism Center at West Point.

9. Imam Shaheed Hassan Al-Banna, The *Way of Jihad: Complete Text by Hassan Al-Banna founder of the Muslim Brotherhood, http://actmemphis.org/MB-The-Way-of_Jihad-by-al-Banan.pdf.* (retrieved 5/08/2017)

10. Al Shaheed Sayyid Quib, 1964, *Milestones*, Azzam Publications; 2nd, Revised edition May 1, 2001 (retrieved 9/08/2017) ttp://www.kalamullah.com/Books/milestones.pdf. (Retrieved 9/08/2017)

11. Shaykh 'Abdullah Yusuf 'Azzam, *"Ilhaq bil-Qafilah"* (Join the *Caravan*) (retrieved 11/05/2017)*https://archive.org/details/opensource&sort=-reviewdate?and[]=subject%3A%22Jihad%22.*

12. Ibid. *Bin Laden's 1996 Declaration of War against US.*

13. Ibid. *Bin Laden's 1996 Declaration of War against US.*

14. Ibid. *Bin Laden's 1996 Declaration of War against US.*

15. Sahih Bukhari, Vol.1, Book: 2, Number 25 Hadith, translation by Dr. M., Muhsin Khan. http://sahih-bukhari.com/Pages/Bukhari_1_2.php (Retrieved 11/10/2017)

16. Sahih Al-Bukhari, Hadith, Volume 4, Book 52, Number 256, Narrated by As-Sab bin Jaththama, http://sahih-bukhari.com/Pages/Bukhari_4_52.php (Retrieved 12/22/2017)

17. Sahih Al-Bukhari, Hadith, Volume 4, Book 52, Number 256, Narrated by As-Sab bin. http://www.answering-islam.org/Responses/Abualrub/terorism2.htm. (Retrieved 11/21/2017)

APPENDICES

"AFGHANISTAN AND THE CALL FOR A GLOBAL JIHAD: HOW DID THE WAR IN AFGHANISTAN PRODUCE THE CALL FOR A JIHAD AGAINST THE WEST?"

By: Professor. Anna Mae D. Simmons

Arab proverb, *"The enemy of my enemy is my friend, to destroy my enemy but they are still my enemy."*

Chinese proverb, *"It is good to strike the serpent's head with your enemy's hand,"*

The invasion of Afghanistan by the Soviet Union in 1979 opened the door that had been closed since 1258, when the Mongols destroyed Baghdad, the political and cultural center of the Muslim Abbasid dynasty. It gave the Muslim fundamentalists an opportunity to finally make their cause a global call for justice and unite the Muslims throughout the world into one unified group, the "Ummah." An old Arab adage, "The enemy of one's enemy could be your potential ally" defines the relationship between the war in Afghanistan and the present day threats against the United States and its Western allies. The two super powers, the Soviet Union and the United States, were still at a Cold War standoff. One enemy, the United States, helped them fight against their other enemy, the Soviet Union. They were thus able to solve their present problem with the Soviet Union and leave the door open for a later advancement against the remaining infidel super power, the United States. Hence "The enemy of one's enemy could be your potential ally."

Beginning in 1979 and increasing greatly in numbers by the mid 1980s, thousands of young Arab freedom fighters traveled to Afghanistan to help their fellow Muslim brothers rid their world of one major enemy and superpower, the Soviet Union. It was this very group of young men who formed the first international brigade of the modern Islamist freedom fighters, or the Jihadists global movement. They came largely from Saudi Arabia, Egypt, Palestine, Jordan, Syria, Iraq, Algeria, Yemen, Libya, and Pakistan. They banded together to free Afghanistan from the Soviet Union and to set in motion their long call for a "Universal Islamists Ummah."

They were mostly "Salafists" (1), Muslims who were products of the more radical madrassas (Islamic schools), particularly some of those madrassas in Iran, the "Muslim Brotherhood" (2) schools in Egypt, as well as many of the "Wahhabi" (3), which are spread over the Muslim world. They had one goal—to fight the infidels face to face as real Jihadists, not as Arab/Muslim soldiers of apostate regimes. This call for a Jihad (struggle) had been silently issued for hundreds of years since the Prophet's return to Mecca and has been even more prominent since the fall of the Islamic empire in the late eleventh and early twelfth centuries. Also with the collapse of the Ottoman Empire and the sultanate in 1923 following WWI, their ultimate goal has been to reinstate the "Caliphate" (4). The Muslims have not had one true Caliph since the collapse of the Ottoman Empire. It was these young freedom fighters in Afghanistan, dedicated to their prestigious past, who looked for and needed a martyrdom or victory to prove that Allah was with them in their battle for a Universal Islamic Ummah. The Afghanistan war and the defeat of one enemy super power, the Soviet Union, gave these young fighters the prestige and face saving that their Islamic community had lost hundreds of years ago.

It is important to note that these young volunteers, who were the Arab "freedom fighters" and were known as the "Arab Afghans," later became the core of the fighting machine known as the al-Qaeda. During the cold war, most Arab regimes, particularly those who had an alliance with the Soviet Union, such as Syria, Iraq, Algeria, Sudan, and Yemen, mistrusted their Arab Afghans. They were also problematic for the pro-American governments such as Jordan, Egypt, Morocco, Tunisia, Saudi Arabia, and Kuwait. But the United States government had a sustained policy of support to the "Mujahidin" (5) in Afghanistan and the international allies who came to fight with them.

As long as the Cold War was still in effect, the Jihad terrorist was a secondary priority for the United States and their Western allies. The United States perceived these young Islamist Jihadists as an objective ally against the Soviet Union. The U.S. intelligence and its government agencies failed to acknowledge that the international call for a Jihad was a separate entity from the war in Afghanistan, since once the Jihadists had defeated one super power they would turn against the remaining super power, even if it had helped them obtain this defeat. "The enemy of one's enemy could be your potential ally." Basically, what happened is that events moved much faster than the evolution of western understanding. The former "Jihadist allies" in the struggle against the Soviet Union did not wait long before they launched their new Jihad against the United States and their allies. "Ihna asqatna al soviet!" (We brought the Soviets down) "la mish ibna Allah asquat al Soviet!" (No, not us, Allah brought the Soviets down)

This quote from Bin Laden and the Taliban following the defeat of the Soviet Union in Afghanistan should have sent a signal to the United States and the Western powers of what was to be their new challenge in the 1990s and beyond. This one statement, made by Bin Laden, revealed both the political and religious thinking of the new Arab Afghans and their call for a Jihad. Their victory over the Soviet Union proved to the "Arab Afghans" or Jihadists that Allah was with them and they could not lose. Who defeated the Soviets in Afghanistan? For these young Muslim fighters the answer to this question was very simple. The Jihadists did and Allah was their ally and the "power" that allowed it. With Allah in their favor "no one" could defeat them. It was the perfect time to take their Jihad global. A question frequently asked by the public in both the United States and the Western nations was: "Why did the Soviet Union collapse immediately after it was defeated in Afghanistan?" In the minds of the young "Arab Afghans" who fought so hard in Afghanistan, the fall of the Soviet Union was "not" due to a failure of the Soviet economy, but rather to the use of "one enemy against another." Allah had blessed them and helped them destroy the infidel

Soviet Union—one of the most dangerous atheist nations in the world. This very powerful but simple reasoning by the Jihadist was missed or ignored by the United States and other Western nations. For the Jihadist this was the perfect time to reopen their call for an international Jihad and the return of the "Islamic Ummah."

If a war against one's enemy can be led by the "right people," following the Qur'an, the Sunnah/Hadith, and the Shari'ah laws, and if it is sanctioned by an Islamic cleric, and it is at the "right time", then Allah would secure their victory. The Islamist Jihadists are confident that they are the "right people" and now is the "right time." The downfall of the Soviet Union validated this belief and convinced them that they could attack and defeat any enemy of Islam, no matter how powerful and influential they were. The United States and its allies would automatically be the next project on their list. Everything the Jihadists were doing pleased Allah; therefore, they could not lose. Allah had given a pure victory to his own fighters and therefore proved to the world, not only to the Muslims, that no power on earth, not even a super power like the Soviet Union or the United States, can defeat a Jihad.

What led to the attack on 9/11 and the terrorist attacks since the war in Afghanistan was not based primarily on economic and geopolitical factors, but on religious beliefs. For the terrorists who have called for a Global Jihad, their logic and goals are totally based on theological reasoning, which may seem irrational to some scholars. Yet this is the primary motivation of the Islamist Jihadists and they are convinced of the undeniable support of Allah in their present call for a Global Jihad.

The current goal of the Islamist Jihadists is defeating the United States the exact same way they defeated the Soviet Union in Afghanistan. "The enemy of one's enemy could be your potential ally."

Who might that enemy be?

Post Script to article -

The most infamous individual who came out of the alliance and the war in Afghanistan is Usama Bin Laden. Many people have written about his life history, his family wealth, his education, his speeches, the horrendous terrorist attacks for which he was responsible, and his mesmeric abilities to recruit young followers. But what is really important are his visions, his strategies, and the reasoning behind what he does. A study of his leadership skills and abilities and how he used them is of course of interest, but what is most crucial to the United States government is the impact he has had on the Jihadist, their movements, and the generations who are following him.

1. Salafist - Individuals who believe that all the events which took place in the formation and early years of Islam are true and are explained by the power given to the Caliph or founding fathers. The more they followed these founding fathers the more Allah would bless them and grant them great victories over their enemies

2. Muslim Brotherhood—Founded in Egypt in the early 1920s, the Muslim Brotherhood has produced some very radical Islamic Fundamentalists. Noted for their complex and covert organizational structure and strategies, they were founded under political suppression and are one of the most feared terrorist organizations today.

   • Mitchell, Richard P., *"The Society of the Muslim Brothers"*, New York, Oxford University Press, 1993. Perhaps one of the best books written that reveals the Muslim Brotherhood organization.

3. Wahhabi—derived from Ibn Abd al-Wahhab, the founder in the eighteenth century of a movement known as Wahhabism. He was a scholar, a jurist, and a writer in the province of Najd in Saudi Arabia. There are fourteen large volumes comprising his writings and commentaries. The image many people have of Wahhabism is a movement of violent and extremely militant followers. However, a close study of Ibn Abd al-Wahhab writings reveals a more moderate teaching which emphasized education, missionary work, charitable giving, women's rights, as well as limitations on violence

and killings. The Wahhabi Madrassas are Islamic schools that are founded on the Qur'an and religious teachings of Islam. It is the belief of many scholars throughout the world that these schools have produced the majority of the mujahidin or Jihadist who have called for a Global Jihad.

4. Caliphate—("Khalifah) Defined in *"A Concise Encyclopedia of Islam"*, by Gordon D. Newby, as the head of the Islamic community in Sunni Islam. The office was regarded as elected, but without a specified process. In the minds of some Muslims, this office was terminated with the capture of Baghdad in 1258 by the Mongols. During the reigns of the first four Caliphs, the shape and duties of the office expanded. Toward the end of the Caliphate, however, the Caliphs were controlled by military rulers, who were given the title Sultan and who kept the Caliphs as virtual puppets to ratify their rule.

5. Mujahidin—Plural for Mujahid one who takes part in a Jihad. They sometimes refer to themselves as Jihadist.

Article published in the Government Security News , May 2010, front page.

CPSIA information can be obtained
at www.ICGtesting.com
Printed in the USA
FFHW021702161218
49899962-54503FF